GUIDE TO
VEGETARIAN
BRIGHTON

Viva! Guide to Vegetarian Brighton
3rd Edition ISBN 0954721659
© Viva! 2006

Compiled by: Jo Lacey
Editor: Juliet Gellatley
Editorial Assistant: Michelle Preston

Printed on recycled paper

Published by Viva!
8 York Court, Wilder Street, Bristol BS2 8QH
Tel: 0117 944 1000
Fax: 0117 924 4646
E: brightonguide@viva.org.uk
W: www.viva.org.uk

Design: Sussed Design – www.susseddesign.com
Cover photo: Corin Jeavons – www.corinjeavons.com
Map by G Scene

Acknowledgements

Thank you to everyone at Viva!, who are working towards ending animal suffering. We'll get there in the end. Your support has been stupendous!

Contents

I hope you find this guide useful and easy to use, here are a few things to bear in mind:

- All the establishments are listed alphabetically and there is a quick reference index at the back of the book.
- Most of the guest houses and hotels are approved by the Tourist Board and can be identified by their diamond or star ratings. Diamonds are awarded to guest houses and B&Bs and stars are the equivalent for hotels. The highest award is five.
- The prices given for the hotels are on a per person, per night basis unless otherwise stated.
- The percentages given for vegetarian and vegan food are rough guidelines. Restaurants are constantly amending their menus. Obviously Viva! can't take responsiblity for any changes!

Introduction – The Place to Be!

Brighton – it's the place to be. Look on any bus and it will tell you so. Ask any clubber and they'll agree. Survey summer trippers and they'll give the idea a big thumbs up.

But the place to be what? For decades it was the place to be naughtily sexy, as generations of lovers, their hormones throbbing, headed to the sea for anonymity and amour. If you couldn't afford Paris then Brighton was a good second choice.

The Prince Regent started the trend, sowing his regal wild oats amid the splendour of his Nash-designed Royal Pavilion. A Disneyesque composite of Oriental styles which never really existed – a fantasy to rival Disney World but conceived and executed before Walt ever drew a breath. And it's all still here so step inside and savour the decadence. The beauty of the music room, the splendour of the dining hall and the opulence of the drawing rooms was how Prinny impressed his conquests.

For the lesser monied who flocked to the sea after him, eager to bask in his reflected glory, it was a chip supper, a squeaky mattress and breakfast sharp at eight. Perhaps it still is.

Brighton is the place not to obey authority and people steadfastly refuse to call it Brighton & Hove, despite the council's efforts. But the feeling is mutual so those that live on the other side of the floral clock will never fail to remind you of where they come from – Hove, actually.

Brighton is the place to be a raver with probably the best selection of clubs in one small area after Ibiza. It's the place to be an antiquarian, poking around the Lanes looking for bargains and never finding any – but having a wonderful time nevertheless. And it's the place which inflicted a plague on the rest of the country – the knockerboys. Door to door antique buyers with their own brand of communication: No love, it's a pile of old tat but I'll take it off your hands for a tenner!

It's the place to be a perpetual student, arriving to take a degree at one of the two universities and never leaving, eventually becoming a website designer. Clydeside had its shipbuilders, Brighton has its website designers.

With more pubs than you can shake a stick at, it's the place to experience a little of Graham Greene's 1930s Brighton Rock sleaze. Sit quietly in a corner seat in dozens of the little back street drinkers and you'll still hear Pinky throwing his weight around, preparing to take on the London mob.

Brighton is a place to be yourself. If you want to walk down the street looking like Carmen Miranda, wear a ball gown, tights and flippers or sell the Big Issue with a tap dance routine, this is the place to do it – and no one will even look twice at you.

But above all Brighton is the place to be a vegetarian. What other town's most popular up-market restaurant is veggie? Where else would you find an entirely veggie pub? And in what other town could you gain discounts of up to 25 per cent off restaurant bills by being a member of a great, campaigning, national vegetarian and vegan group – a group

that is succeeding in its determination to save animals?
Where else but Brighton! Viva! Brighton! Viva! Viva!.

Tony Wardle
Tony Wardle is a journalist, writer and associate director of Viva!

(V) on the menu examples denotes a vegan dish.

The Viva! Supporter's Discount Scheme

The Viva! Supporter's Discount Scheme is set up to enable
you to obtain discounts at various establishments.
All you have to do is join Viva! (see page 117 for details) and
as soon as you've received your supporter's card away you go
getting up to 25 per cent discounts. Look out for the special
icon ✔ telling you which places offer a Viva! discount. For a
full discount list covering the whole of the UK (including
guest houses, hotels, restaurants, cafes, pubs and shops)
phone Viva! on 0117 944 1000, email angie@viva.org.uk or
log on to www.viva.org.uk/businesses/discountlist.

Quick Guide to Vegetarian Establishments in Brighton and Key to Map on pages 8-9

1   Bombay Aloo
2   The Cowley Club
3   The End of the Lanes Café
4   Food for Friends
5   The George
6   The Guarana Bar
7   Infinity Foods Café & Take-Away
8   Planet India
9   RedVeg
10 Seasons of Lewes
11 Terre à Terre
12 Vegetarian Shoes
13 Wai Kika Moo Kau

P   Parking
i   Tourist Information

Also see page 110 for index of 90% or more vegetarian establishments

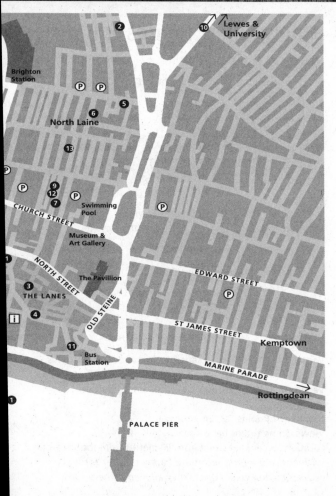

Lewes &
University

Brighton
Station

North Laine

CHURCH STREET

Swimming
Pool

Museum &
Art Gallery

The Pavillion

NORTH STREET

THE LANES

OLD STEINE

EDWARD STREET

ST JAMES STREET

Kemptown

MARINE PARADE

Rottingdean

Bus
Station

PALACE PIER

Hotels, Guest Houses & B&Bs

Abbey Lodge ★★★

19 Upper Rock Gardens, Brighton BN2 1QE
Tel: 07980 643049
E: abbeybrighton@aol.com
W: www.abbeybrighton.com

Guest House
Price: £30 - £50
Breakfast: Special diets are catered for – so just let them know if you're veggie.
Number of Rooms: 4; **En Suite:** 2
Views: Some rooms have oblique sea views.
Location: Two minutes from town and the sea side.

Adastral Hotel ◆◆◆

8 Westbourne Villas, Hove BN3 4GQ
Tel: 01273 888800
E: adastral@mistral.co.uk
W: www.adastralhotel.co.uk

Hotel
Price: £62.50 - £85
Veggie Breakfast: Veggie sausages, tomatoes, mushrooms, baked beans, eggs (as you like), cereals, porridge, omelettes.
Vegan Breakfast: Porridge, baked beans, tomatoes, mushrooms.
Number of Rooms: 23; **En Suite:** 21
Views: Some rooms have a sea view.
Location: On a quiet street just 200 metres from the sea front.
With notice the proprietors are happy to cater for vegetarian and vegan diets. They allow __pets__ here too.

Ainsley House ◆◆◆◆

28 New Steine, Brighton BN2 1PD
Tel: 01273 605310
E: rooms@ainsleyhotel.com
W: www.ainsleyhotel.com

Grade II Town House Hotel

Price: £30 - £45

Veggie Breakfast: Cereals, yoghurt & fresh fruit, eggs, beans, tomatoes, veggie sausages or omelettes.

Vegan Breakfast: Soya milk available. Fresh fruit, veggie sausages, beans, tomatoes.

Number of Rooms: 11; **En Suite:** 8

Views: Back rooms have a view of the garden, front rooms look over the sea, garden square and Brighton Pier.

This is an excellent hotel with a pleasant ambience and high standards. It's also very central and in a pretty spot.

Ambassador Hotel ◆◆◆◆

22-23 New Steine, Brighton BN2 1PD
Tel: 01273 676869
E: info@ambassadorbrighton.co.uk
W: www.ambassadorbrighton.co.uk

Hotel

Price: £30 - £95

Vegan Breakfast: Tofu & vegetable sausages, tomatoes sprinkled with basil & olive oil, mushrooms, beans & hash browns with fair trade organic tea, coffee and hot chocolate.

Number of Rooms: 34; **En Suite:** 24

Views: Some rooms have sea views.

Location: Close to town and the sea.

Arlanda Hotel ◆◆◆◆

   20 New Steine, Brighton BN2 1PD
   Tel: 01273 699300
   E: arlanda@brighton.co.uk
   W: www.arlandahotel.co.uk

Hotel
Price: £42 - £60
Veggie Breakfast: Yoghurt, eggs, tomatoes, mushrooms & beans, muffins and croissants or fresh fruit.
Vegan Breakfast: Cereals, fresh and dried fruit, mushrooms, tomatoes & beans.
Number of Rooms: 16; **En Suite**: 15
Views: The garden square and Brighton Pier.
Situated just off the sea front and very central, this hotel offers a warm welcome for everyone.

Ascott House Hotel ◆◆◆◆

   21 New Steine, Brighton BN2 1PD
   Tel: 01273 688085
   E: welcome@ascotthousehotel.com

Guest House
Price: £40 - £50
Veggie Breakfast: Veggie English breakfast or pancakes with maple syrup, home-made banana milkshakes, fresh fruit or eggs in the format of your choice!
Number of Rooms: 15; **En Suite**: 10
Views: The front rooms look out to the sea, Brighton Pier and a regency square.

Bannings Guest House

> 14 Upper Rock Gardens, Brighton BN2 1QE
> Tel: 01273 681403
> E: info@bannings.co.uk
> W: www.bannings.co.uk

Bed & Breakfast

Price: £42 - £48 for a double room

Veggie Breakfast: Veggie/vegan sausage, hash brown, tomato, mushrooms & scrambled eggs.

Vegan Breakfast: As above with beans instead of eggs. Soya and wheat milks are available.

Number of Rooms: 6; **En Suite**: All en suite or with a shower room.

This gay-friendly establishment offers a great vegan brekkie and is just a few minutes from the sea front.

The Belgrave ★ ★ ★ ★

> 64 Kings Road, Brighton BN1 1NA
> Tel: 01273 323221
> W: www.thebelgravehotel.com

Hotel

Price: £85+

Veggie Breakfast: Full veggie English breakfasts are available.

Vegan Breakfast: The Belgrave are happy to cater for vegans with prior warning.

Number of Rooms: 63; **En Suite**: 63

Views: 44 of the rooms have sea views.

This hotel is in central Brighton and right on the sea front. They have recently refurbished the beautiful Victorian building and it looks great. Seasons Café Bar is attached (see page 43) as well as The Belgrave Café Bar.

Berkeley House Hotel

2 Albion Street, Lewes BN7 2ND
Tel: 01273 476057

Bed & Breakfast

Price: £37.50 - £65

Veggie Breakfast: Cereals, fruit juices, fresh fruit, toast, free-range eggs, grilled tomatoes & baked beans.

Vegan Breakfast: As above (without the eggs). Soya milk and soya margarine are available.

Number of Rooms: 5; **En Suite**: Yes

Views: The top room has views across Lewes to the Downs. Two rooms look out across the garden and two look across the street.

Berkeley House is a Georgian town house in a quiet street in the centre of Lewes. Booking is advisable but there is a charge. You can rest assured that your brekkie will be GMO-free.

Beynon House ◆◆◆

24 St George's Terrace, Brighton BN2 1JJ
Tel: 01273 681014
E: beynonhouse@hotmail.com
W: www.beynonhouse.co.uk

Guest House

Price: £25 - £30

Veggie Breakfast: Vegetarian sausages, hash browns, eggs (as you like them), mushrooms, tomatoes & beans.

Vegan Breakfast: Fresh fruit or mushrooms, beans or tomatoes on toast. Non-dairy spread is available.

Number of Rooms: 7; **En Suite**: 7

Views: Situated in a Victorian terrace in the heart of Kemptown. *You'll get a good night's sleep in this quiet street and a generous breakfast.*

Boydens

27 St James' Avenue, Brighton BN2 1QD
Tel: 01273 601914
E: boydens@brightonrock.co.uk
W: www.brightonrock.co.uk
Bed & Breakfast
Price: £25 - £40
Veggie Breakfast: Omelettes or scrambled eggs or eggs,
tomatoes, mushrooms, fried potatoes & baked beans.
Vegan Breakfast: As above without the eggs.
Number of Rooms: 6; **En Suite**: Most en suite or with showers.
Views: Victorian terrace in a tree-lined street.
Comfortable, clean and cosy with a TV and tea and coffee
facilities in every room.

Brighton Backpackers

75-76 Middle Street, Brighton BN1 1AL
Tel: 01273 777717
E: backpackers@fastnet.co.uk
W: www.brightonbackpackers.com
Beds and Self-catering Facilities
Price: £13 - £30
En Suite: In double rooms only.
Views: Sea view with double rooms.
A fun-packed crazy place for international travellers and
students, located in the centre of town with a relaxed and
friendly atmosphere (no curfew). Internally it has painted
murals and cartoon characters throughout. There are social
areas with good hi-fi, satellite television, pool table and
even music while you shower. Choose from staying in a
dormitory or double room with a sea view and get cheap
rates for water sports, roller-blading and bike hire.

Brighton House ◆◆◆◆

> 52 Regency Square, Brighton BN1 2FF
> Tel: 01273 323282
> E: enquiries@brightonhousehotel.co.uk
> W: www.brightonhousehotel.co.uk

Guest House
Price: £35 - £40
Veggie Breakfast: Buffet style – cereals, fresh fruit, eggs, toast, muffins, cheeses.
Number of Rooms: 14; **En Suite**: 14
Views: Overlooking Regency Square and oblique sea views from some rooms.
The Brighton House offers a warm and friendly welcome to this recently renovated grade II listed building. Near the West Pier, the town centre is a brief walk away. Just two rules – no children and no smoking.

The Cavalaire ◆◆◆◆   ✔ 5%

> 34 Upper Rock Garden, Brighton BN2 1QF
> Tel: 01273 696899
> E: welcome@cavalaire.co.uk
> W: www.cavalaire.co.uk

Bed & Breakfast
Price: £29 - £145
Veggie Breakfast: Vegetarian English breakfast with Linda McCartney sausages or a tropical fruit concoction.
Vegan Breakfast: By prior arrangement.
Number of Rooms: 11; **En Suite**: 11
Views: No particular views.
Book online for this reasonably priced, non-smoking, pleasant B&B.

Cecil House Hotel ♦♦

126 Kings Road, Brighton BN1 2FA
Tel: 01273 325942
E: info@cecilhotel.co.uk
W: www.cecilhotel.co.uk

Bed & Breakfast

Price: £35 - £140

Veggie Breakfast: Full continental including croissants, yoghurt, fresh fruit, toast & muffins.

Number of Rooms: 12; **En Suite:** 4

Views: Some sea views.

A small and friendly B&B opposite the West Pier.

The Dudley Hotel ★★★

Landsdown Place, Hove BN3 1HQ
Tel: 01273 736266
E: admin@thedudleyhotel.co.uk
W: www.thedudleyhotel.co.uk

Hotel

Price: £65+

Veggie Breakfast: Cereals, fruit compots, yoghurts and a hot buffet including hash browns, tomatoes, beans & mushrooms.

Vegan Breakfast: Can provide soya milk with prior warning. Various items from the hot buffet and cereals available.

Number of Rooms: 71; **En Suite:** 71

The Dudley Hotel is a traditional Victorian building and has been awarded three stars by the Tourist Board. The town centre is a 10-15 minute walk away or a quick bus ride.

Fyfield House Hotel ◆◆◆◆

26 New Steine, Brighton BN2 1PD
Tel: 01273 602770
E: fyfield@aol.com
W: www.brighton.co.uk/hotel/fyfield

Guest House
Price: £50 - £100
Veggie Breakfast: Cereal, yoghurt, fruit, toast, egg, tomatoes, mushrooms, beans, hash browns & veggie sausage (home-made).
Vegan Breakfast: As above (without the yoghurt and eggs) with scrambled tofu available. They also provide vegan spread and soya milk.
Number of Rooms: 9; **En Suite**: 6
Views: Views of the sea and gardens.
Fyfield House is a private hotel they describe as a home from home. The hotel is two minutes away from the sea front and a pleasant stroll away from shops, theatres, pubs and clubs. One of the rooms has a four-poster bed. Peter and Anne are willing to cater for vegetarians and vegans, just let them know in advance what your needs are and they'll do their best to meet them. They've got a garden hot tub for you to relax in, look at the stars and sup a glass of wine.

Genevieve Hotel ◆◆◆◆

18 Madeira Place, Brighton BN2 1TN
Tel: 01273 681653
W: www.genevievehotel.co.uk

Hotel
Cost: £45 - £95
Veggie Breakfast: Continental – croissant, fruit & cereals.
Number of Rooms: 13; **En Suite**: 13

Just a one minute walk away from the sea front and Brighton Pier, this guest house is clean, comfortable, friendly and bright.

The Granville Hotel ★ ★ ★

124 Kings Road, Brighton BN1 2FA
Tel: 01273 326302
E: info@granvillehotel.co.uk
W: www.granvillehotel.co.uk
Hotel - Bed & Breakfast or Full Board
Price: £42.50 - £77.50
Veggie Breakfast: Full organic vegetarian breakfast – veggie sausage, veggie bacon, fried bread etc, cereals or fresh fruit salad.
Vegan Breakfast: Vegan sausage, scrambled tofu, mushrooms, fruit, cereals etc. Soya margarine and soya milk are always available.
Number of Rooms: 24; **En Suite:** 24
Views: Rooms are individually designed and most have a view of Brighton sea front and the West Pier. Some rooms have antique four-poster beds, jacuzzis or waterbeds.

Grapevine

29-30 North Road, Brighton BN1 1YB
Tel: 01273 703985
E: enquiry@grapevinewebsite.co.uk
W: www.grapevinewebsite.co.uk
Accommodation with cafe attached
Price: £13 - £30
Number of Rooms: 15; **En Suite:** 0
Views: Street.
Located on a North Laine main road and very close to the

station. The Grapevine is ideal for parties. They welcome hens and stags to their shared rooms for up to 10!

Gullivers Guest House
   10 New Steine, Brighton BN2 1PB
   Tel: 01273 695415
Bed & Breakfast
Price: £36+
Veggie Breakfast: Full English (with Linda McCartney sausages).
Vegan Breakfast: Continental or as above without eggs.
Number of Rooms: 20; **En Suite:** Mostly
Views: Some rooms have a sea view.
Central and very near the sea front and the Palace Pier.

Harvey's Guest House ♦♦♦ ✔ 10% (off 3 nights or more)
   1 Broad Street, Brighton BN2 1TJ
   Tel: 01273 699227
Guest House
Price: £25 - £45
Veggie Breakfast: Cereals and fruit, eggs, beans & tomatoes or fried egg on toast with fried potatoes, grilled tomatoes, mushrooms & beans. Bloody Marys available for those in desperate need!
Vegan Breakfast: Vegan sausages, tomatoes & beans (soya milk and marg available).
Number of Rooms: 7; **En Suite:** 7
Views: Oblique sea views for the front rooms and roof tops for the rear rooms.
Great location near the sea front, shops and Brighton Pier.

Hilton West Pier & Hilton Metropole ★ ★ ★ ★

106-121 Kings Road, Brighton BN1 2FU
Tel: 01273 329744/775432 Phone 0990 909090 to book
E: reservations.brightonmet@hilton.com
W. www.hilton.co.uk
Bed & Breakfast or Full Board
Price: £45 - £190
Veggie Breakfast: Buffet breakfast – minimum 12 hot items and 8 cold items.
Vegan Breakfast: As above – soya milk available.
Number of Rooms: 334; **En Suite:** 334
Views: Some rooms have sea views, others of the hotel roof.
These two hotels are situated a mere 200 yards apart along the sea front and are central. Both are magnificent, glamorous and suitable for a very special occasion. The Metropole is a major function venue in the UK. The restaurant is large, bright and overlooks the sea – a good place for a celebration. The vegetarian options are imaginative and high quality. If you're a vegan let them know before you go and they'll give you some options. The dishes are à la carte for example – Wild Mushroom Stroganoff in Filo Pastry, Sesame, Herb & Wild Rice Tofu Burgers (V), Char-grilled Aubergines with Vegetable Parcels, Vegetable Strudel on a Spring Onion & Corriander Creme. Three course menu £17.95.

Hotel Pelirocco ♦♦♦♦

10 Regency Square, Brighton BN1 2FG
Tel: 01273 327055
E: info@hotelpelirocco.co.uk
W. www.hotelpelirocco.co.uk
Hotel

Price: from £50 - £260
Number of Rooms: 19; **En Suite**: 18
Veggie Breakfast: Full veggie including sausages, egg, tomato, mushrooms & beans or scrambled cheesey egg on toast or cinnamon toast.
Vegan Breakfast: Full veggie breakfast minus the egg or beans/mushrooms on toast. Soya milk is available.
Views: Of Regency Square, the sea and the West Pier.
If you're after somewhere special then this is the place. The rooms are themed around pop subculture or provoked by visionary artists, maverick musicians and inspired individuals. Choose from the sexy space age room to the romantic absolute love room.

Hotel Seafield ♦♦♦

23 Seafield Road, Hove BN3 2TP
Tel: 01273 735912
Bed & Breakfast (evening meal if required)
Price: £40+
Veggie Breakfast: Eggs as you like them, tomatoes, mushrooms & sauté potatoes or a mushroom omelette, cereals and toast.
Vegan Breakfast: Tomatoes, mushrooms, sauté potatoes & baked beans with toast. Soya margarine and milk are available.
Number of Rooms: 14; **En Suite**: 12
Views: The front rooms overlook the tree-lined street and the back rooms, the garden.
*Just on the edge of the main shopping centre, this B&B is close to the King Alfred Leisure Centre and the sea front. A big bonus is the free private parking and that **pets** are allowed.*

Hudsons ◆◆◆◆

22 Devonshire Place, Brighton BN2 1QA
Tel: 01273 683642
E: info@hudsonshotel.com
W: www.hudsonshotel.com

Guest House
Price: £45 - £105
Veggie Breakfast: Cereals and fruit or a full veggie English with toast & home-made marmalade or other spreads.
Vegan Breakfast: Adapted from above. With prior notice they are happy to cater for vegans.
Number of Rooms: 9; **En Suite**: 5
Hudsons is owned by two vegetarians who cater primarily for gay and lesbian guests. This cosy, converted 19th century town house offers clean comfortable rooms and ample breakfast.

Kingsway Hotel ◆◆◆◆

2 St Aubyns, Hove BN3 2TB
Tel: 01273 722068

Bed & Breakfast
Price: £30 - £75
Veggie Breakfast: Poached eggs, scrambled eggs on toast, veggie sausages.
Vegan Breakfast: Can accommodate vegans with prior notice.
Number of Rooms: 20; **En Suite**: Many
Views: Sea views from many rooms.
Near the sea front in Hove and very near to the King Alfred Leisure Centre, for a slightly quieter time than the central B&Bs.

Lichfield House ♦♦♦

30 Waterloo Street, Brighton BN3 1AN
Tel: 01273 777740 / 07970 945464
E: feelgood@lichfieldhouse.freeserve.co.uk
W: www.lichfieldhouse.freeserve.co.uk

Hotel/Bed & Breakfast
Price: £25 - £40
Veggie Breakfast: Omelettes or eggs on toast, croissants, currant buns or cereals.
Number of Rooms: 8; **En Suite**: 5
This B&B is a brief walk from the sea front and the West Pier. The rooms are individually designed to be stylish, tasteful and colourful. The have treatment rooms offering aromatherapy, sports massage and reflexology.

Marina House Hotel ♦♦♦

8 Charlotte Street, Brighton BN2 1AE
Tel: 01273 605349
E: rooms@jungs.co.uk

Bed & Breakfast
Price: £19 - £45
Veggie Breakfast: Choose from a continental or traditional veggie English start to the day.
Vegan Breakfast: Continental or scrambled egg-less with tomatoes & mushrooms. Soya milk and margarine are available.
Number of Rooms: 10; **En Suite**: 7
Located in a quiet side street just out of the hustle and bustle of the town – but an easy walk back to it! Each room is imaginatively decorated and themed – some have four-poster beds.

Oriental Hotel ♦♦♦

9 Oriental Place, Brighton BN1 2LJ
Tel: 01273 205050
E: info@orientalhotel.co.uk
W: www.orientalhotel.co.uk

Hotel
Price: £35 - £125
Veggie Breakfast: Full vegetarian breakfast or muesli with fresh fruit & yoghurt.
Vegan Breakfast: Veggie sausages, mushrooms (cooked in olive oil), tomatoes, beans & toast or muesli with fresh fruit. They are happy to provide soya milk with advance warning!
Number of Rooms: 12; **En Suite**: 8
Views: Two of the rooms have balconies and views of the sea, the others overlook the street.
This hotel is very relaxed and friendly. The food is organic and the coffee is fairly traded. The have a massage therapist and acupuncturist available should you need it.

Palace Hotel ♦♦♦

10-12 Grand Junction Road, Brighton BN1 1PN
Tel: 01273 202035

Hotel
Price: £30 - £55
Veggie Breakfast: Full vegetarian selection (veggie sausages, mushrooms, tomatoes, eggs & fried bread) or cereals.
Number of Rooms: 28; **En Suite**: 28
Views: The sea front and Brighton Pier.
Although they don't cater for vegans this handy hotel is just around the corner from Terre à Terre (see page 71) and the Lanes.

Palm Court

371 Kingsway, Hove BN3 4QD
Tel: 01273 417821

Bed & Breakfast
Price: From £15 per person per night
Veggie Breakfast: Eggs, beans, tomatoes, mushrooms & toast or cheese on toast.
Vegan Breakfast: Beans, tomatoes & mushrooms on toast.
Number of Rooms: 5; **En Suite**: None
Views: Two rooms have sea views.
Open all year round 24 hours a day. Not very central, but buses are frequent and cheap into town.

Paskins Town House ♦♦♦ ✔ 20% (excluding weekends)

18-19 Charlotte Street, Brighton BN2 1AG
Tel: 01273 601203
E: welcome@paskins.co.uk
W: www.paskins.co.uk

Hotel
Price: £27.50 - £65
Veggie Breakfast: The full vegetarian breakfast consists of home-made veggie sausages (with sun-dried tomatoes, tarragon & paprika), fritters, corn sauce, eggs, tomatoes, mushrooms & toast. Or you could have the Brighton Rarebit which is vegetarian cheese toasted on organic wholemeal bread with tomato & mushroom.
Vegan Breakfast: Vegans are welcome and well catered for with soya milk and margarine always available.
Number of Rooms: 19; **En Suite**: 16
Views: Like Paris!
Mostly local organic produce used to create the full-on breakfasts and you can wash them down with fair trade tea,

coffee or hot chocolate. This hotel was built around 1800 and the rooms have a sort of Edwardian theme. A few minutes walk from the Palace Pier and the Lanes and very near the sea front.

Penny Lanes ♦♦♦♦

11 Charlotte Street, Brighton BN2 1AG
Tel: 01273 603197
E: welcome@pennylanes.co.uk
W: www.pennylanes.co.uk

Bed & Breakfast

Price: £30 - £89

Veggie Breakfast: Choose from the full veggie – eggs (as you like), local farm veggie sausages, tomatoes, mushrooms, beans & a potato waffle or a fluffy omelette.

Vegan Breakfast: Full vegan breakfast with soya milk available on request.

Number of Rooms: 11; **En Suite**: 6 (but all have showers)

This is a really lovely, homely and friendly B&B which I heartily recommend. It's a stroll from the centre of town and near the sea front.

Sea Spray ♦♦♦

25 New Steine, Brighton BN2 1PD
Tel: 01273 680332
E: seaspray@brighton.co.uk
W: www.seaspraybrighton.co.uk

Guest House

Price: £22.50 - £40

Veggie Breakfast: Veggie sausage, hash browns, egg, mushroom, tomato, beans & toast or cereals and fruit juice.

Vegan Breakfast: Two vegan sausages, beans, mushrooms,

tomatoes & toast or cereals. Soya milk and soya spread
are available.
Number of Rooms: 8; En Suite: 8
Views: Half the rooms overlook the garden square and
Brighton Pier.
*One of the rooms is particularly special with a four-poster
bed and French doors opening on to a balcony.*

Topps Hotel ♦♦♦♦

17 Regency Square, Brighton BN1 2EG
Tel: 01273 729334
W: www.brighton.co.uk/hotels/topps
Hotel
Price: £40 - £129
Veggie Breakfast: Seasonal fruit and cereals or eggs, veggie
sausage, tomatoes, mushrooms & beans.
Vegan Breakfast: As above without the eggs.
Number of Rooms: 15; En Suite: 15
Views: The large double rooms overlook Regency Square,
the West Pier and the sea.
*For extra cosiness the double rooms have gas coal fires along
with four-poster beds and balconies. Topps Hotel offers a
warm, friendly service.*

The Twenty One Hotel ♦♦♦♦

21 Charlotte Street, Marine Parade, Brighton BN2 1AG
Tel: 01273 686450/681617
E: the21@pavilion.co.uk
W: www.chelsoft.demon.co.uk/21.htm
Bed & Breakfast
Price: £35 - £150
Veggie Breakfast: Full vegetarian breakfast or juices and cereals.

Vegan Breakfast: Full vegan breakfast. Soya milk and margarine available.
Number of Rooms: 8; **En Suite**: 8
Views: Some rooms have partial sea views.

Located in a quiet side street, just a few steps from the beach, the Twenty One is an early Victorian town house. They offer many special breaks, such as a trip to France, or a Christmas treat. Vegetarians and vegans are well catered for with a separate menu. The Twenty One claims to be the best B&B in Brighton. It is well worth visiting their website for a look at the individually designed rooms, some with four-poster beds.

Willow Guest House

37 Russell Square, Brighton BN1 2EF
Tel: 01273 326129
Bed & Breakfast
Price: £25 - £50
Veggie Breakfast: Vegetarian English breakfast with vegetarian sausage or scrambled egg on toast/continental style.
Number of Rooms: 10; **En Suite**: 3
Views: Front views over Russell Square Gardens.
*Situated between the main shopping area and the sea front. A recently refurbished Regency building offers a cosy retreat where **dogs are welcome** by arrangement.*

Restaurants, Cafés & Pubs
Central Brighton

Akash Tandoori (Restaurant)

26 Preston Street, Brighton BN1 2HN
Tel: 01273 324494

Type of Cuisine: Indian
Breakdown: (out of 100 dishes) Vegetarian: 40%; Vegan: 10%
A wide selection of vegetable curries on offer – so if curry is what does it for you then go to Akash. Choose from hot, hotter or stupidly hot! As with all Indian cuisine, it's best to order lots of dishes and share them.
Vegetable Korma £3.95, Vegetable Malayan £3.95, Vegetable Balti £5.95, Tarka Dahl £2.55
Opening Hours: Monday - Saturday noon - 3pm & 6pm - midnight Sunday noon - midnight

Al Rouche (Restaurant)

44 Preston Street, Brighton BN1 2HP
Tel: 01273 734810

Type of Cuisine: Lebanese and Continental
Breakdown: (out of 40 dishes) Vegetarian: 10%; Vegan: 5%
There are plenty of veggie starters to be had, so I recommend ordering a selection of starters to share. The look of this restaurant is very authentic and the food is traditional.
Batata Hara (potatoes with coriander, herbs & garlic) £2.95, Tabouleh £2.95
Opening Hours: Monday - Thursday 8am - 10pm Friday & Saturday 8am - 10.30pm Sunday from 9am - 10pm

Bombay Indian Cuisine (Restaurant)

86-87 Preston Street, Brighton BN1 2HQ
Tel: 01273 721199/203228

Type of Cuisine: Indian
Breakdown: (out of 100 dishes) Vegetarian: 25%; Vegan: 10%
The Bombay is fully air conditioned so even if your tonsils are screaming you can keep your cool. It's a large restaurant so it's a good place to go if there's a big party of people. Their wide variety of dishes – from vegetable bhoona to sag aloo – are selected from all regions of India to spice up your life.
Vegetable Biriani £5.95, Vegetable Madras £3.95, Masala Papadum 70p, Onion Bhaji £2.45
Opening Hours: Monday - Saturday noon - 2.30pm & 6pm - midnight Sunday noon - midnight

Brighton Bystander (Café)

1 Terminus Road, Brighton BN1 3PD
Tel: 01273 329364

Type of Cuisine: Breakfasts and Hot Snacks
Breakdown: (out of 200 dishes) Vegetarian: 40%; Vegan: 10%
The Bystanders are Brighton's very own greasy spoons. They have a good range of vegetarian and vegan dishes – both clearly labelled.
Veggie Gut Buster (veggie burger, veggie sausage, egg, beans, tomato, mushrooms & chips) £5.50, Vegan Breakfast £3.60
Opening Hours: Every day 8am - midnight

Casalingo (Restaurant)

29 Preston Street, Brighton BN1 2HP
Tel: 01273 328775

Type of Cuisine: Italian
Breakdown: (out of 40 dishes) Vegetarian: 15%; Vegan: 0%

The vegetarian dishes are clearly marked on this menu.
Casalingo has a funky and modern feel.
Penne al Pesto £5.50/£8.50, Carrot & Coriander Soup £3.95,
Cannelloni di Magro (with spinach & ricotta cheese) £5.50/£8.50

The Cous Cous House (Restaurant)

10 Preston Street, Brighton BN1 2HN
Tel: 01273 323230

Type of Cuisine: Moroccan
Breakdown: (out of 30 dishes) Vegetarian: 20%; Vegan: 15%
*This stands out amongst the other restaurants on Preston
Street because it's offering something very different. Those
little balls of pasta we know as cous cous are coupled with
rich and fragrant sauces to create delicious dishes. Choose
from traditional Moroccan seating with low sofas and round
tables or your more 'normal' table and chairs option. There's
also a belly dancer on Friday and Saturday nights.*
Carrot Salad £3.50, Cous Cous & Vegetables in Saffron Sauce
£8.95, Tagine Vegetable £8.95, Moroccan Mint Tea £2.25
Opening Hours: Monday - Saturday noon - 2.30pm
Monday - Thursday 6pm - 11pm
Friday & Saturday 6pm - midnight
Sunday noon - 3pm & 6pm - 10.30pm

Dig in the Ribs (Restaurant)

47 Preston Street, Brighton BN1 2HP
Tel: 01273 325275

Type of Cuisine: Mexican
Breakdown: (out of 35 dishes) Vegetarian: 30%; Vegan: 0%
*I was pleasantly surprised to find a selection of vegetarian
dishes at a place called Dig in the Ribs – I thought it would
be cow pie all round! In fact the dishes are tasty and the*

restaurant has a spacious, new-style Mexican theme. Give it a go Gringo! Although nothing listed on the menu is vegan they can adapt the dishes to suit your needs.

Chimichanga (large crisp burrito topped with guacamole, salsa & sour cream) £10.25, Nachos with Sour Cream & Guacamole £4.65/£7.95, Sunshine Salad (star fruit, kiwi, melon, mango, pineapple & orange on a garden salad with pine kernels & cashews) £7.95

Opening Hours: Monday - Saturday noon - 11pm
Sunday noon - 10.30pm

Good Friends (Restaurant)

25 Preston Street, Brighton BN1 2HN
Tel: 01273 779836/774193

Type of Cuisine: Chinese
Breakdown: (out of 70 dishes) Vegetarian: 20%; Vegan: 15%
Authentic Chinese food served in a spacious venue with large round tables that are perfect for getting to chat to everyone you're dining with.

Crispy Seaweed £3, Vegetable Spring Roll £2.95, Vegetable Singapore Noodles £3, Deep-fried Bean Curd in Chilli & Salt £4

Opening Hours: Every day noon - midnight

Havana (Restaurant)

32 Duke Street, Brighton BN1 1AG
Tel: 01273 773388

Type of Cuisine: Modern Gourmet
Breakdown: (out of 21 dishes) Vegetarian: 10%; Vegan: 5%
From the outside Havana looks quite small, but once you're in through the doors it opens into palatial splendour. A grand piano, large plants and a waterfall set the scene for culinary delights. Exquisite, innovative cuisine awaits you.

Risotto of Parsnip with Smoked Tomato Chutney, Rocket Salad & Gespachio Sauce £6.50, Organic Tofu Marinated in Soya Sauce & Sesame Seeds, Kataifi Balls Stuffed with Goat's Cheese & Celeriac on a Potato Rosti with a Salad of Noodles, Wasabi & Pinapple Yoghurt £12.50

Opening Hours: Every day noon - 5pm & 7pm - 11pm

Jason's (Take-Away)

50 North Street, Brighton BN1 1RH
Tel: 01273 220254

Type of Cuisine: Sandwiches and Pastries
Breakdown: (out of 100 dishes) Vegetarian: 30%; Vegan: 10%
Jason's can make sandwiches to order and serve fresh soup during the winter months. There are lots of veggie pasties and vegan samosas and bhajis.

Spicy Vegetarian Roll 80p, Garlic & Mushroom Pasty £1.10, Hummus & Salad Focaccia (V) £1.60, Cheese & Leek Pasty £1.10, Ricotta, Spinach, Lentil & Tomato Parcel £1.10, Homity Pie £1.10, Various Soups £1.50 (with Roll), Jamaican Pasty (V) £1

Opening Hours: Monday - Saturday 7am - 6.30pm
Sunday 11am - 6pm

Jethro's (Café/Take-Away)

35 Queen's Road, Brighton BN1 3XB
Tel: 01273 325888
W: www.jethros.co.uk

Type of Cuisine: Global
Breakdown: (out of 50 dishes) Vegetarian: 20%; Vegan: 5%
A fantastic range of vegetarian take outs or food for delivery, even picnic boxes, useful as it's on the way from the train station to the beach – ideal for many visitors. You can even have your Sunday lunch delivered.

Grilled Halloumi, Mediterranean Vegetables & Spiced Cous Cous £3.95, Mushroom Risotto £2.35, Salads including tabbouleh, coleslaw & mixed leaves and home-made puddings like Apple Pie, Chocolate Mousse and Tiramisu.
Opening Hours: Every day 5.30pm - 10.30pm

Kambi's (Restaurant)

107 Western Road, Brighton BN1 2AA
Tel: 01273 327934
Type of Cuisine: Lebanese
BYO
Breakdown: (out of 60 dishes) Vegetarian: 50%; Vegan: 15%
Loads of vegetarian options to eat in or take out. The falafel & hummus in pitta bread with tahini sauce is a delicious take-away. Look out for the prawn & vegetable curry in the vegetarian main course section – I think it's a red herring!! To eat in this restaurant really captures a Middle Eastern atmosphere with the a heady blend of arabic spices and music.
Warakinab (vine leaves stuffed with rice, tomato, herbs & spices) (V) £2.50, Moussaka Batinjan (fried aubergine with chickpeas, tomatoes & spices) £2.50, Sambousak (pastry filled with cheese, onion & pine nuts) £2.75, Loubieh (french beans with tomato & garlic) £2, Batahara (potatoes cooked in olive oil with spices & garlic) £2
Opening Hours: Monday - Saturday noon - midnight
Sunday noon - 11.30pm

Guide to Vegetarian Brighton

Mr Grints (Sandwich Bar)

13 Cranbourne Street, Brighton BN1 2RD
Tel: 01273 728091

Type of Cuisine: Sandwiches and Pasties

Breakdown: (out of 80 dishes) Vegetarian: 20%; Vegan: 5%

Choose to sit in or out or take away from this handy sandwich shop. The vegan pasties are really tasty and leave poppy seeds stuck in your teeth, making interesting afternoon nibbles! There are also plenty of vegetarian pasties to choose from.

Vegan Friendly Roasted Vegetables Five Bean Hummus Sandwich (V) £2, Vegan Friendly Poppy Seeded Pasty (V) £1.20. Also a selection of crisps, drinks and fruit are available.

Opening Hours: Monday - Friday 7.30am - 5.30pm
Saturday 8am - 6pm Sunday 8am - 5pm

Paris Texas American Bistro (Restaurant)

128 Western Road, Brighton BN1 2AD
Tel: 01273 747111
E: usabistro@aol.com

Type of Cuisine: Tex-Mex

Breakdown: (out of 50 dishes) Vegetarian: 35%; Vegan: 25%

Live life to the full American style at Paris Texas where big portions and lots of flavour are the key to success. Vegetarians and vegans are well catered for. Choose from tortillas, fajitas or chimichanga and enjoy the taste of America.

Deep-fried Potato Skins with Sour Cream, Salsa & Guacamole £2.75, Courgette, Aubergine & Tomato Fajitas £8.95, Spicy Vegetable Burrito & Chimichanga £7.25, Californian Salad (greens topped with avocado, nuts, olives, raisins & orange) £7.25

Opening Hours: Sunday - Thursday 11am - 10pm
Friday & Saturday 11am - 11pm

Pizza Hut (Restaurant)

81-82 Western Road, Brighton BN1 2HA
Tel: 01273 327991
& 2 Dyke Road, Brighton BN1 3FE
Tel: 01273 328666

Type of Cuisine: Pizza/Pasta
Breakdown: (out of 20 dishes) Vegetarian: 25%; Vegan: 0%
The cheese on the pizzas is vegetarian – hooray! However they don't offer any vegan dishes, apart from the salad bar of course.
Country Feast Pizza £5.49/£8.49/£10.99, Vegetable Pasta Bake £5.50, Garlic Bread £1.80/£2.20 (with cheese)
Opening Hours: Sunday - Thursday noon - 10pm
Friday & Saturday noon - 11pm

Planet India (Restaurant)

54 Preston Street, Brighton BN1 2HE
Tel: 01273 275717

Type of Cuisine: Indian
Breakdown: (out of 50 dishes) Vegetarian: 100%; Vegan: 80%
Preston Street's restaurants can take you all over the world but India really is the god-father (or should that be Buddha-father?!) of vegetarian food. Planet India brings you authentic, home-made Indian food, made by authentic home-made Indians. They love cooking up the delicious curries and it really shows in their mouth-watering dishes. For just £3.90 you can feast on their curry & rice and at such a bargain you'd be forgiven for thinking you were in India.
Opening Hours: Tuesday - Saturday noon - 3pm & 6pm - 10pm
Closed Sunday & Monday

Real Patisserie

43 Trafalgar Street, Brighton BN1 4ED
Tel: 01273 570719

Type of Cuisine: Sandwiches, Quiches and Pastries
Breakdown: (out of 60 dishes) Vegetarian: 30%; Vegan: 5%
The yellow and purple décor gives a fresh, clean and funky feel to this patisserie. There are quite a few savoury lunch options, but beware of the gelatine in some of the cakes and tarts. They sell great organic breads which are vegan.
Vegetarian Mini Pizza 90p, Spanish Omelette (slice) £1.40, Quiche Vegetarienne £1.30, Organic Seeded Loaf £1.15, Walnut & Rye Bread £1.05
Opening Hours: Monday - Saturday 7.45am - 5.30pm

The Thai Garden (Restaurant)

81-82 Preston Street, Brighton BN1 2HG
Tel: 01273 772211

Type of Cuisine: Thai
Breakdown: (out of 90 dishes) Vegetarian: 15%; Vegan: 10%
Take your taste buds back-packing through Thailand, Peking and Japan with this menu. There's a good selection of veggie starters but we miss out on the main dishes so it's a good idea to order lots of starters and share them.
Tempura Vegetables £3.50, Deep-fried Crispy Seaweed £2, Mee Krob (crispy fried noodles & dry bean curd paper with sweet tomato sauce) £3, Vegetable Spring Rolls £2
Opening Hours: Tuesday - Sunday noon - 11.30pm

Thai Orchid (Restaurant)

65 Preston Street, Brighton BN1 2HE
Tel: 01273 323224

Type of Cuisine: Thai
Breakdown: (out of 60 dishes) Vegetarian: 40%; Vegan: 30%
With the authentic figurines and pictures you could be forgiven for thinking you were in Thailand. If that doesn't convince you then the food surely will.
Spring Rolls £3.95, Tempura Puk £3.95, Priew Wan Pug (sweet & sour vegetables) £4.50, Tofu Gra-Pow £5.50, Thai Green Curry £4.95
Opening Hours: Monday - Sunday 12.30pm - 4pm (except Tuesday) & 5.30pm - 11pm

Western Front (Pub)

11 Cranbourne Street, Brighton BN1 2RD
Tel: 01273 725656

Type of Cuisine: Various
Breakdown: (out of 20 dishes) Vegetarian: 25%; Vegan: 5%
Stylish and funky with orange walls and good vegetarian options right near Churchill Square shopping centre makes for a handy snack stop.
Vegetable Spring Rolls with Sweet Chilli Dipping Sauce £2.75, Haloumi, Hummus & Salad in a Wrap £4.25, Vegetarian Sausages with Kabli Channa £5.50
Opening Hours: Monday - Saturday noon - 7pm
Sunday noon - 6pm

The Sea Front

The Boardwalk (Restaurant/Bar)

250a Kings Road Arches, Brighton BN1 1NB
Tel: 01273 746067

Type of Cuisine: Global
Breakdown: (out of 22 dishes) Vegetarian: 40%; Vegan: 0%

The Boardwalk is a converted deckchair pavilion, just west of Brighton Pier. Sit outside and you're right next to the beach. The interior is stylish and fresh – much like the food which is also GM-free and free-range/organic where possible. Fresh juices, shakes and smoothies are available (and I don't mean the bar staff!).

Bangers & Mash £4.80, Pasta Funghi £4.95, Vegetable Stir-fry £5.80, Char-grilled Halloumi (oven-roasted peppers stuffed with halloumi & feta cheese) £4.95

Opening Hours: Every day 8am - 11pm

Due South (Restaurant)

139 Kings Road Arches, Brighton BN1 2FN
Tel: 01273 821218
W: www.duesouth.net

Type of Cuisine: Global
Breakdown: (out of 30 dishes) Vegetarian: 30%; Vegan: 15%

Due South source their ingredients from local, organic, free-range producers. The menu is seasonal so expect something different with each visit. Their motto is simple – honest and delicious food – and they certainly deliver. The coffee and chocolate they sell is fairly traded so feel free to indulge. Choose from al fresco seating or the cosy, relaxed indoor area.

Feta, Sweetcorn & Spring Onion Fritters with Roasted

Tomato £7.50, Soup & Bread £3.95, Lentil Salad (V) £2.25, Goat's Cheese Salad with Cherry Plum Tomatoes & Red Peppers £7.50, Jerusalem Artichoke & Parmesan Tart with Ragout of Winter Vegetables £11.50, Elderflower & Vanilla Pannacotta with Rhubarb Compote £5.50
Opening Hours: Every day noon - 4pm & 6pm - 10pm

The Honey Club (Bar/Café/Club)

214 Kings Road Arches, Brighton BN1 1NB
Tel: 01273 202807
W: www.thehoneyclub.co.uk
Type of Cuisine: Café Style and Specials
Breakdown: (out of 30 dishes) Vegetarian: 8%; Vegan: 0%
Sea front bar by day and club by night, The Honey Club is close to town and Brighton Pier. It's always packed during summer days.
Amorini & Stilton Bake £4.75, Mushroom Stroganoff £4.75, Char-grilled Veggie Burger £3.75. The menu also includes sandwiches and jacket potatoes.
Opening Hours: noon - late

Louis' Beach Café

163 Kings Road Arches, Brighton BN1 1NB
Tel: 01273 771555
Type of Cuisine: Café Snacks and Smoothies
Breakdown: (out of 10 dishes) Vegetarian: 10%; Vegan: 0%
What could be nicer when you've over-heated on the beach than a pineapple, kiwi, strawberry & orange smoothie? The menu is simple and quite limited, but if you're after a quick drink or snack it's perfect.
Fresh Fruit Smoothies £2.50, Home-made Cakes £1.20, Cinnamon Toast £1.20, Cream Cheese & Chive Bagel £3
Opening Hours: 8am - 7pm

The Plaza (Restaurant)

43-45 Kings Road, Brighton BN1 1NA
Tel: 01273 232222
W: www.plaza-brighton.co.uk
E: enquiries@plaza-brighton.co.uk

Type of Cuisine: Various
Breakdown: (out of 25 dishes) Vegetarian: 10%; Vegan: 0%
The Plaza may look a bit pricey at first glance, but as well as your meal you get a beautiful sea view and live music on Friday and Saturday nights. The large dining area includes optional seating outside overlooking the sea. If you really like it you can stay and drink cocktails until 2am.
Roasted Red Pepper & Basil Soup £3.65, Watermelon & Feta Cheese Salad with Toasted Pumpkin Seeds & Tomato Dressing £3.95, Stuffed Peppers £8.95
Opening Hours: Every day 10am - late

Redz (Bar/Brasserie)

The Old Ship Hotel, Kings Road, Brighton BN1 1NA
Tel: 01273 329001

Type of Cuisine: English and Continental
Breakdown: (out of 40 dishes) Vegetarian: 10%; Vegan: 0%
A bright, stylish brasserie with a rich warm décor and a contemporary mood on the sea front with the vegetarian options clearly marked on the menu.
Char-grilled Vegetable Ciabatta £4.50, Potato Gnocchi served with Gorgonzola & Garlic Cream Sauce £6.50, Japanese Tempura Vegetables with a Sweet Chilli Dipping Sauce £6.50, Sticky Toffee Pudding £4.50
Opening Hours: Monday - Saturday noon - 11pm
Sunday noon - 10.30pm

Seasons Café Bar

64 Kings Road, Brighton BN1 1NA
Tel: 01273 323221

Type of Cuisine: International

Breakdown: (out of 30 dishes) Vegetarian: 5%; Vegan: 0%

Cool down after lazing on the beach all morning in this air conditioned, stylish café bar. Feast on hot ciabatta sandwiches while you watch the world whizz by along the sea front.

Hot Ciabatta Sandwiches filled with Roasted Peppers, Brie, Sun-dried Tomatoes & Light Pesto Mayonnaise £5, Chick Pea Burger & French Fries £5.50, Tortellini Formaggio (with fresh oregano, garlic, cream & ciabatta bread) £6.95

Opening Hours: Every day 12.30pm - 9.30pm

North Laine

The Bagelman (Take-Away)

7 Bond Street, Brighton BN1 1RD
Tel: 01273 387171
E: bagels@bagelman.co.uk

Type of Cuisine: Deli-Style Bagels
Breakdown: (out of 20 dishes) Vegetarian: 75%; Vegan: 50%
The Bagelman is Brighton's one and only authentic bagel bakery. Cooked on the premises by hand throughout the day, they are absolutely delicious and totally animal-free. You can have whatever you fancy in your bagel (within reason)! They also make different flavoured bagels like cinnamon & raisin, onion & poppy seed – yum!
Veggie Feast (hummus, cheddar/Swiss cheese, avocado, onion, tomato, cucumber & lettuce) £2.10, Mighty Aphrodite (feta, tomato, olives & basil) £2.10 Falafel in Pitta (V) £2.40/£2.60 with Hummus
Opening Hours: Monday - Saturday 8am - 5pm
Sunday 10am - 4pm

Bill's @ The Depot (Café)

100 North Road, Brighton BN1 1YE
Tel: 01273 692894
W: www.billsproducestore.co.uk

Type of Cuisine: Café
Breakdown: (out of 40 dishes) Vegetarian: 50%; Vegan: 10%
This converted warehouse will wow you with its speciality exotic and unusual foods. A new and popular addition to the North Laine eateries, with a menu to make you drool!
Bill's Vegetarian Breakfast (toast, poached egg, tomatoes,

home-made hummus, avocado, mushrooms & sweet chilli sauce) £6.95, Grilled Vine Tomatoes on Toast £5.25, Salad Plate & Foccacia £7.25. They try and accommodate vegans and have soya milk available.
Opening Hours: Monday - Saturday 8am - 6pm
Sunday 10am - 4pm

Café Laziz

48 Gardner Street, Brighton BN1 1UN
Tel: 01273 625544
Type of Cuisine: Sandwiches and Snacks
Breakdown: (out of 30 dishes) Vegetarian: 30%; Vegan: 10%
This is a great spot to get a quick feed and watch the world go by through the big windows at the front of the café. Although the menu is pretty basic the hearty portions make this place worth a visit.
Vegetable Samosa £1.25, Slice of Pizza £1.50, Hummus & Falafel Wrap (V) £2.50, Home-made Vegetable Lasagne £3
Opening Hours: Every day 9am - 6pm

Café Nia

87-88 Trafalgar Street, Brighton BN1 4ER
Tel: 01273 671371
Type of Cuisine: Up-Market Café
Breakdown: (out of 40 dishes) Vegetarian: 30%; Vegan: 5%
This is stylish and rustic, posh and basic all at once and in all the right places. The big glass windows give you a feeling of spaciousness and the deep colours inside make you feel cosy. The simple, elegant food is cooked fresh so they can easily adapt a meal to make it vegan. They also are GM-free and use a lot of organic products including the eggs and cheese.
Ciabatta Stuffed with Avocado, Mozzarella & Olive Oil £4.95,

Butternut Squash Risotto Drizzled with Olive Oil & Shaved
Parmesan £7.50, Pan-fried Gnocchi with Gratinated
Courgettes, Ricotta & Roasted Tomatoes £10.25, Caramalised
Apple Brulee £4.95
Opening Hours: Monday - Saturday 9am - 11pm
Sunday 9am - 6pm

Capers (Café)

27 Gardner Street, Brighton BN1 1UP
Tel: 01273 675550

Type of Cuisine: All Day Breakfast and Hot Snacks
Breakdown: (out of 30 dishes) Vegetarian: 20%; Vegan: 0%
Choose from a veggie breakfast, sandwich or jacket potato
if you fancy a snack or alternatively tuck into veggie
bangers & mash.
Vegetarian Home-made Soup £1.90/£2.60 with Bread, Veggie
Bangers & Mash with Onion Gravy £5.10, All-Day Veggie
Breakfast £4.50, Scrambled or Fried Eggs & Beans on Two
Slices of Toast £2.65
Opening Hours: Tuesday - Saturday 9am - 5.30pm
Sunday 10am - 3pm

Crumbs (Café)

22 Bond Street, Brighton BN1 1RD
Tel: 01273 620806

Type of Cuisine: Sandwiches/Snacks
Breakdown: (out of 70 dishes) Vegetarian: 30%; Vegan: 10%
Plenty of veggie sandwiches available here as well as more
exciting options. This place has a bright feel and everything
is cooked fresh. The soup of the day is always vegetarian.
Vegetarian Sausage Sandwich £1.85, Salad Pots
(risotto/potato salad) £1.50, Lentil Soup £1.80, Veggie

Breakfast £4.20, Pizza £2.80
Opening Hours: Monday - Saturday 8am - 5.30pm
Sunday 11am - 4pm

Domino's Pizza (Take-Away)

16-17 St George's Place, Brighton BN1 4GB
Tel: 01273 675676

Type of Cuisine: Pizzas
Breakdown: (out of 70 dishes) Vegetarian: 50%; Vegan: 25%
*Domino's Pizza will tailor make a pizza just for you. If you
don't want cheese they can smother your pizza in garlic and
stack up the toppings. And you can have your munchies
delivered to your door.*
Garlic Bread £1.95, Vegetarian Supreme £4.25 - £12.25
depending on size, Chocolate Mousse £1.50
Opening Hours: Every day noon - 10pm (carry out)/
11pm (delivery)

The Dorset (Café/Bar)

28 North Road, Brighton BN1 1YB
Tel: 01273 605423

Type of Cuisine: Various
Breakdown: (out of 50 dishes) Vegetarian: 20%; Vegan: 5%
*A large stylish bar on the corner of North Road. The staff are
friendly and in the summer it's a real treat to sit outside and
watch the world go by. They offer slightly unusual bar food
and enough vegetarian choices to make it worth a visit. The
food is GM-free and free-range/organic where possible.*
Veggie Full House (breakfast) £6.25, American Pancakes with
Maple Syrup £4.75, Crepe Malcolm (pancake with garlic,
mushrooms, spring onions, matured stilton & baked tomato)
£7.45, Sunday Veggie Roast £5.95

Opening Hours: Monday - Friday 11am - 10pm
Saturday & Sunday 10am - 10pm

The Dumb Waiter (Café)

28 Sydney Street, Brighton BN1 4EP
Tel: 01273 602526

Type of Cuisine: Light Snacks and Meals
Breakdown: (out of 80 dishes) Vegetarian: 30%; Vegan: 10%
The sassy orange walls and the packed in furniture give this place a cosy feel. The large window enables you to watch the wildlife of Brighton go by while creating steamy images with your mug of tea. The Dumb Waiter has a huge menu for such a small place. One of the best veggie breakfasts in town is on offer as well as loads of other great veggie dishes. I highly recommend the chai served here.
Vegan Breakfast (sausage, bubble & squeak, beans & tomatoes) £3.50, Jacket Potato with Mushrooms £2.70, Veggie Sausage Sandwich £1.80, Pitta with Hummus & Falafel £2.50, Vegan Nut Burger £2.40
Opening hours: Monday - Saturday 9am - 5pm
Sunday 10am - 3.30pm

El Mexicano (Restaurant)

7 New Road, Brighton BN1 1UF
Tel: 01273 727766
E: elmexicano@youtopia.co.uk
W: www.elmexicano.co.uk

Type of Cuisine: Mexican
Breakdown: (out of 40 dishes) Vegetarian: 45%; Vegan: 10%
Having been to Mexico I can assure you that this food is really authentic. With a recent face-lift, El Mexicano is now looking more traditional too, with soft lighting and a

romantic feel. A lot of the dishes are made with cheese but they are happy to make vegan versions.

Quesadillas (warmed flour tortilla, folded in half, filled with cheese & mushroom) £2.75, Nachos with Cheese, Jalapenos & Salsa £3, Enfrijoladas (fried tortillas bathed in a black bean sauce) £5.95

Opening Hours: Sunday - Thursday noon - 11.30pm
Friday & Saturday noon - midnight

Fringe (Bar/Café)

10 Kensington Gardens, Brighton BN1 4AL
Tel: 01273 623683

Type of Cuisine: Light Snacks and Meals
Breakdown: (out of 40 dishes) Vegetarian: 50%; Vegan: 20%
There's a lovely balcony over Kensington Gardens which is a great sun trap and a perfect spot to watch the world go by. There's plenty for veggies and good vegan options on the menu and a good balance between burgers and fried breakfasts and healthier options. The soup of the day is always vegan.

Omm Burger with Mockney Oink (home-made vegetarian nut burger with vegan bacon, relish, side salad & chips) (V) £5.95, Veggie Hot Dog with Caramelised Onions & Mustard £4.50, Veggie Breakfast £4.75, Home-made Porridge with Fresh Fruit & Soya Milk £3.50

Opening Hours: Monday - Friday 11am - 8pm
Saturday & Sunday 10.30am - 9pm

The George (Pub/Restaurant)   ✔ 25% (off food)

5 Trafalgar Street, Brighton BN1 4EQ
Tel: 01273 681055

Type of Cuisine: Global Vegetarian and Vegan
Breakdown: (out of 50 dishes) Vegetarian: 100%; Vegan: 75%
A firm fave of me and my pals. And if you have a Viva!
Supporter's card you get a generous 25 per cent discount here
on the massive portions of well made cuisine. The seasonal
menu adapts with your dietary needs throughout the year,
offering lighter meals in the summer and hearty grub for the
winter. Check the blackboard for the daily specials. There is a
designated dining area which is smoke-free and child friendly.
The pub is filled with dark chunky wooden tables with
benches or chairs and you can choose to be tucked away in
one of the nooks or right in the thick of it near the large bar.
Vietnamese Baguette (mushroom pate, marinated julienne
vegetables in a fresh baguette/focaccia served with salad &
fries) (V) £5.45, Veggie Bangers & Mash (V) £5.95, Falafels
Platter (V) £6.15, Mediterranean Vegetable Wrap (V) £5.95
Opening Hours: Monday - Thursday noon - 9.30pm
Friday - Sunday noon - 8pm

The Guarana Bar (Café/Juice Bar)   ✔ 10%

36 Sydney Street, Brighton BN1 4EP
Tel: 01273 621406
E: jk@guarana.demon.co.uk
W: www.goguarana.com

Type of Cuisine: Juice, Shakes and Smoothies
Breakdown: (out of 15 dishes) Vegetarian: 100%; Vegan: 90%
Whether you want to get that natural high, cleanse your
system or get a vitamin boost you can choose the shake or
juice to suit you. Geared up as a pre-club bar-shop, the legal

the george

vegan & vegetarian

f o o d

brighton's only vegan & vegetarian pub
quality food menu, changed regularly
booking can be made for ten or more

the george, 5 trafalgar st, brighton. 01273 681055

map:
- queen's rd
- brighton station
- sydney st
- trafalgar street
- pelham st
- pelham sq / the george
- brighton tech
- york place
- st. peter's church
- grand parade
- brighton university

heated garden (just replanted)
families welcome
relaxed atmosphere

food: mon–thurs 12–8.30pm
fri–sun 12–7pm
later food times in summer

---

the george

5/06/viva1

25% off *

total food bill with this voucher
applies mon–thurs only

---

the george

5/06/viva1

25% off *

total food bill with this voucher
applies mon–thurs only

---

the george

5/06/viva1

25% off *

total food bill with this voucher
applies mon–thurs only

51

highs are served in a relaxed and friendly space.
Spirulina (for health and vitality) with Wheatgrass (for detoxification) regular £2.20, large £4, Vitamina Shakes (with guarana, banana, honey, yoghurt, milk & ice), regular £2, large £3.60
Opening Hours: Monday - Friday 10.30am - 6.30pm
Saturday & Sunday 10am - 6pm

Infinity Foods Café & Take-Away

50 Gardner Street, Brighton BN1 1UN
Tel: 01273 670743

Type of Cuisine: Organic Vegetarian Delights
Breakdown: (out of 10 dishes) Vegetarian: 100%; Vegan: 60%
A sister to the old favourite, Infinity Foods Shop, this café is a worker's co-operative and serves freshly made organic salads, daily specials, soups, cakes and fair trade tea and coffee to wash them down. You can also get gluten/wheat/sugar free goodies here. The fresh, simple décor certainly suits this contemporary café.
Filled Baps (eg tempeh, tofu, falafel and hummus) £2.95 eat in, £1.65 take out, Vegan Pasty £1.25, Salads Selection £3.95 eat in, £3.05 take out, Daily Special (eg Sweet Potato Rosti with Mediterranean Vegetables) £4.15 eat in, £3.05 take out
Opening Hours: Monday - Saturday 9.30am - 5pm

Inside Out (Café)

95 Gloucester Road, Brighton BN1 4AP
Tel: 01273 692912

Type of Cuisine: Global
Breakdown: (out of 30 dishes) Vegetarian: 30%; Vegan: 15%
The mosaic tables and clay seating area does give you the feeling of being outside when you're in here. It's very fresh

and bright, almost like being on holiday. Children are welcome.

Mixed Berry Smoothie £2.50, Nachos with Salsa, Onion, Avocado, Sour Cream & Olives £4.50, Sun-blushed Tomato, Olive Pesto & Pine Nut Linguine £6.25, Mediterranean Salad (roasted peppers, fennel, tomatoes, red onion & aubergine) £6.25, Carrot Cake (V) £2.75

Opening Hours: Monday - Saturday 8am - 7pm
Sunday 10am - 5pm

I's Pies (Take-Away)

24 Gardner Street, Brighton BN1 1UP
Tel: 01273 688063

Type of Cuisine: Pies!

Breakdown: (out of 20 dishes) Vegetarian: 40%; Vegan: 20%
If you've just spent hours deciding on a purchase in Vegetarian Shoes or if you need pastry sustenance to keep shopping then this is the place to go. They always have a vegan pasty available and I've tried two flavours so far. I'll be performing further sampling before deciding on a favourite though!
Thai Spicy Vegetable Pasty (V) £3, Mediterranean Tomato & Vegetable Pasty £3, Daily Soup (often veggie) £2, Chocolate Cheesecake £1.95. Soya milk available.

Opening Hours: Monday - Saturday 10am - 7pm Sunday noon - 6pm

Kensingtons (Café)

1-2 Kensington Gardens, Brighton BN1 4AL
Tel: 01273 570963

Type of Cuisine: Snacks and Light Meals

Breakdown: (out of 200 dishes) Vegetarian: 30%; Vegan: 10%
Tucked away from the bustling crowds of Kensington

Gardens this café is well worth a visit with plenty for veggies and vegans. Choose from the menu boards which are crammed with sandwiches, jacket potatoes, curries and Mexican dishes, all reasonably priced. Soya milk is available so you can even have a cup of tea!

Breakfast Baguette (fried mushrooms, vegan bacon, vegan sausage, fried tomatoes & baked beans) (V) £3.70, Veggie Chilli £3.50, Fajita Wrap & Chilli £2.95, Avocado Salad Box £3
Opening Hours: Every day 9.30am - 5.30pm

The Off Beat Coffee Bar

37 Sydney Street, Brighton BN1 4EP
Tel: 01273 604206
Type of Cuisine: Sandwiches and Snacks
Breakdown: (out of 25 dishes) Vegetarian: 15%; Vegan: 10%
Totally groovy in a moped-riding, 50s kind of way. It's like going back in time and yet it feels very modern. All the tea and coffee here is fairly traded and they have soya milk.
Veggie Sausage Sandwich £1.90, The Italian Job Toasted Sandwich (mozzarella, pesto & tomato) £2.90, Veggie Breakfast Baguette (veggie sausage, egg, tomato & mayo) £2.50, Soyaccino or Soyalatte £1.40
Opening Hours: Monday - Saturday 10am - 5.30pm
Sunday 11am - 5pm

Oriental Diner (Café/Restaurant)

18 York Place, Brighton BN1 4GU
Tel: 01273 888388

Type of Cuisine: Chinese and English
Breakdown: (out of 150 dishes) Vegetarian: 40%; Vegan: 20%
*This is one of my favourites! You walk through the front
part of the shop which is a chip shop and Chinese take-away
to the back and you are seated in booths. You are then
served authentic Chinese cuisine at very reasonable prices.*
Hot & Sour Bean Curd & Vegetable Soup £1.60, Crispy
Seaweed & Nuts (V) £2.85
Opening Hours: Monday - Saturday noon - 3pm & 6pm -
12.30am Sunday 6.30pm - 12.30am

Pulp Kitchen (Juice Bar/Deli)

31 Bond Street, Brighton BN1 1RD
Tel: 01273 735040

Type of Cuisine: Juices, Soups and Smoothies
Breakdown: (out of 30 dishes) Vegetarian: 70%; Vegan: 40%
*These smoothies and juices will really rock your world.
Whether you want to power up, revitalise, purify, rescue or
feel a bit of passion it's all available on the menu and as for
the shots of wheat grass juice – they're like drinking freshly
mown grass – must be good for you! If you want to give
your immune system a boost, this is the place to do it. They
also sell soups, deli wraps and salads which are clearly
labelled dairy-free, wheat-free vegetarian or vegan. It's also
a very funky place to hang out.*
Mango Tango Juice (mango, passion fruit & orange) £2.50
(medium), Biscotti Beautiful Smoothie (hazelnut, raspberries
& cocoa) £2, Soup (eg carrot & corriander with orange) (V)
£2.50, Blushing Rice (wild rice, tomatoes & roast peppers in a

sun-dried tomato dressing, leaves & parmesan shavings) £2.50
Opening Hours: Monday - Saturday 8.30am - 6pm
Sunday 11am - 4pm

RedVeg (Take-Away/Café)

21 Gardner Street, Brighton BN1 1UP
Tel: 01273 679910
W: www.redveg.com
Type of Cuisine: Veggie Fast Food
Breakdown: (out of 20 dishes) Vegetarian: 100%; Vegan: 80%
This is a great place to go for fast food and if you have any friends on the brink of becoming vegetarian or vegan this will surely push them over the edge. Don't get me wrong, I'm a big lentil lover but hey, just once in a while, a burger and fries are required. Most of the items on the menu can be made vegan to order.
RedVeg Burger £2.85, Spicy Baby Corn Firesticks £1.65, Falafel £3.55, NoName Nuggets £3.25, Large Fries £1.25, Breaded Mushrooms £1.55
Opening Hours: Every day 11am - 9pm

Riki Tik (Café/Bar)

18a Bond Street, Brighton BN1 1RD
Tel: 01273 683844
Type of Cuisine: Light Snacks and Specials
Breakdown: (out of 20 dishes) Vegetarian: 20%; Vegan: 0%
At Riki Tik they use organic and free-range ingredients when available and they provide well for veggies. Make sure you check out the specials board which is nearly two-thirds vegetarian. Riki Tik is also a stylish place to hang out, play Playstation or surf the net and drink cocktails in the evening.
Roasted Organic Vegetables & Hummus in a Floured Wrap

£4.50, Falafel in a Toasted Door Stop Sandwich £4.50, Spicy Veggie Burger served with Fresh Salad & Fries £5.25
Opening Hours: Monday - Sunday 10am - 9.30pm

Sejuice (Café)

56 Gardner Street, Brighton BN1 1UN
Tel: 01273 690035
W: www.sejuice.uk.com

Breakdown: (out of 50 dishes) Vegetarian: 60%; Vegan: 40%
From the outside Sejuice looks like a small juice bar but as you enter it's clearly something quite spectacular. The beautiful front counter will get you drooling and the stylish seating areas that stretch as far as your eye can see are really inviting. Add to this a delicious menu and friendly staff and you've got somewhere pretty special.
Courgette & Yellow Pepper Soup With Bread £2, Fair Trade Capuccino (soya milk available) £2, Japanese Slipper Smoothie (pineapple & mango with freshly squeezed orange juice, low fat frozen yogurt & a dash of lime) large £3.50
Opening Hours: Winter Daily 9am - 5pm Summer Daily 10am - 8pm

Toast (Café)

38 Trafalgar Street, Brighton BN1 4ED
Tel: 01273 626888

Type of Cuisine: Sandwich and Espresso Bar
Breakdown: (out of 40 dishes) Vegetarian: 25%; Vegan: 15%
This place is perfect for commuters (just down the road from the train station). Go here if you're just about to get the morning train up to the big smoke and pick up a couple of toasted crumpets with jam, and when you arrive back in Brighton later you'll be so glad that you need to treat

yourself to a hot chocolate with cream and marshmallows.
Soya milk is available. The sandwich names are fab – it's
worth going just to hear yourself asking for a camel ride in
the middle of winter in Brighton!

Morrissey on Granary (hummus, grated carrot & roast
peppers) £2.30, Camel Ride (falafel, tzatsiki, salad, chilli &
lemon in a wrap) £2.70, Fresh Carrot & Apple Juice £1.70
Opening Hours: Monday - Friday 7.30am - 3.30pm

Wagamama (Restaurant)

Kensington Street, Brighton BN1 4AJ
Tel: 01273 688892
W: www.wagamama.com

Type of Cuisine: Japanese Noodles
Breakdown: (out of 26 dishes) Vegetarian: 23%; Vegan: 12%
As a new and long awaited addition to the Brighton food
scene Wagamama has been welcomed with open arms and is
packed every time I go by. You'll find long benches full of
people scooping up noodles with chopsticks here and I highly
recommend joining them. A good selection for veggies – all
of which can be made suitable for vegans, just ask.

Moyashi Soba (vegetable soup with noodles) (V – if with
udon noodles), Yasai Karroke, Three Potato, Green Pea,
Carrot, Onion & Sweetcorn Cakes with a Sweet Tamarind
Sauce £6.95, Yasai Katsu Curry, Slices of Sweet Potato,
Aubergine & Pumpkin Deep-fried in Crispy Breadcrumbs,
served in a Light Curry Sauce & Japanese-style Rice £6.35
Opening Hours: Monday - Saturday noon - 11pm
Sunday 12.30pm - 10pm

Wai Kika Moo Kau (Café)

11a Kensington Gardens, Brighton BN1 4AL
Tel: 01273 671117

Type of Cuisine: English and Continental
Breakdown: (out of 60 dishes) Vegetarian: 100%; Vegan: 20%
This is a bright and interesting café in the heart of the North Laine. There's seating inside which also spills out on to the street, so you can people watch while enjoying a hearty breakfast, a healthy lunch or afternoon tea.
Tempura Japanese Style Vegetables £6.25, Mushroom Ravioli £5.45, Veggie Breakfast £3, Veggie Burger with Fries & Salad £4.95, Veggie Bangers & Mash £5.95
Opening Hours: Monday - Sunday 9am - 6pm

Yum-Yum Noodle Bar (Café)

22-23 Sydney Street, Brighton BN1 4EN
Tel: 01273 606777

Type of Cuisine: Malaysian, Thai, Chinese and Indonesian
Breakdown: (out of 30 dishes) Vegetarian: 33%; Vegan: 10%
Yum-Yum is upstairs from an oriental supermarket, both of which are charming dens of unusual and exotic foods. The selection includes mock duck which is quite a spooky taste sensation.
Noodles, Rice & Spring Roll £4.85, Singer Noodle Nasi Goren (V) £4 - £5
Opening Hours: Monday - Thursday noon - 6pm
Friday noon - 6pm
Saturday noon - 6pm Sunday noon - 5.30pm

The Lanes

Ask (Restaurant)

58 Ship Street, Brighton BN1 1AF
Tel: 01273 710030

Type of Cuisine: Italian
Breakdown: (out of 40 dishes) Vegetarian: 20%; Vegan: 10%
Popular chain, the décor is striking, ultra modern and spacious. They serve mainly pasta, pizzas and salads; classic Italian with a gourmet touch. Top quality. The toilets are stylish too – well worth a visit! The pizzas can be made without cheese for a vegan version, but the pasta dishes are made with egg pasta.

Pizza Vegetariana £6.50, Spaghetti al Pomodoro £5.30, Mushrooms al Forno (baked mushrooms stuffed with parmesan, garlic & breadcrumbs) £3.75, Penne con Pomodori Secchi (sun-dried tomatoes, artichokes, basil, chillies & olive oil) £6
Opening Hours: Every day noon - midnight

Blind Lemon Alley (Restaurant)

41 Middle Street, Brighton BN1 1AL
Tel: 01273 205151

Type of Cuisine: American
Breakdown: (out of 20 dishes) Vegetarian: 20%; Vegan: 10%
Here you will find a relaxed warm welcome and cool blues tucked away in an almost secret location – well not anymore! With live music on Sunday nights and generous portions this is an ideal place to sample home-made burgers among the best in Brighton.

Baked Mushrooms Stuffed with Garlic Savoury Butter £5.95,

Lentil Burger (home-made with guacamole) £7.95
Opening Hours: Every day noon - late

Bombay Aloo (Restaurant)

39 Ship Street, Brighton BN1 1AB
Tel: 01273 776038

Type of Cuisine: Vegetarian Indian Buffet
Breakdown: (out of 15 dishes) Vegetarian: 100%; Vegan: 60%
Bombay Aloo has a bistro feel and offers a buffet of 15 tasty vegetarian dishes many of which are vegan – so you can pick and choose. There are plenty of pickles and sauces as well as naan to enhance the flavours of India. Help yourself again and again until you're fit to burst. This popular restaurant is excellent value.

Vegetarian Indian Buffet £4.95
Opening Hours: Sunday - Thursday noon - 11pm
Friday & Saturday noon - midnight

Café Rouge (Restaurant)

24 Prince Albert Street, Brighton BN1 1HF
Tel: 01273 774422

Type of Cuisine: French
Breakdown: (out of 30 dishes) Vegetarian: 10%; Vegan: 0%
Café Rouge is a nice restaurant in a pretty part of town. There are enough vegetarian dishes to make you feel welcome, but they are way too cheesy for vegans.

Deep-fried Camembert with Red Currant Sauce £4.85, Penne Pasta with Asparagus, Courgette, French Beans & Spinach in a Herb, Cream & White Wine Sauce £7.65, Brie & Spinach Torte £7.95, Goat's Cheese Salad £7.45, Roasted Vegetable Torte £6.95
Opening Hours: Monday - Saturday 9am - 11pm
Sunday 10am - 10.30pm

Casa Don Carlos (Restaurant)

5 Union Street, Brighton BN1 1HA
Tel: 01273 327177

Type of Cuisine: Spanish Tapas ('the little dishes of spain')
Breakdown: (out of 50 dishes) Vegetarian: 10%; Vegan: 0%

Just like its food this restaurant is traditional, well-prepared and aromatic. On a sunny day in Brighton you really could convince yourself you were in Spain with the red and white checked table cloths and Spanish music. The food is spicy and pretty cheap. You can mix and match your dishes – or ideally share with your mates.

Berengenas Fritas (deep-fried aubergine) £3.30, Garbanzos con Espinacas (chickpeas with spinach) £3.35, Chilli Potatoes £3.20
Opening Hours: Monday - Friday noon - 3pm & 6pm - 11pm
Saturday & Sunday noon - 11pm

The Coach House (Restaurant/Bar)

59a Middle Street, Brighton BN1 1AL
Tel: 01273 719000
E: coachhousebar@aol.com
W: www.coachhousebrighton.com

Type of Cuisine: Global
Breakdown: (out of 35 dishes) Vegetarian: 20%; Vegan: 10%

Spacious, rustic setting with a beautiful fire in the middle of the restaurant area. The Coach House is very popular so get there early for a good seat and book on the weekends. The vegetarian options are clearly labelled on the menu and there's vegan food too – just ask. Keep an eye out for the specials blackboard.

Traditional Italian Layered Aubergines £8.95, Portabella Mushrooms £9.95, Coach House Salad £6.95, Thai Red Curry £6.95, Tempura, Vegetable & Noodle Salad £5.95, Vegetarian

Bangers & Mash (lunchtimes only) £6.95, Nut Roast (Sundays only) £7.95, Walnut, Mushroom & Dochelate Noisetine with Beetroot & Horseradish Salsa Wrapped in a Puff Pastry Parcel (Sundays only) £8.95
Opening Hours: Monday - Saturday 11am - 11pm
Sunday 11am - 10.30pm

The End of the Lanes Café

53 Meeting House Lane, Brighton BN1 1HB
Tel: 01273 729728

Type of Cuisine: Premium Coffee and Pastries
Breakdown: (out of 10 dishes) Vegetarian: 100%; Vegan: 5%
Possibly the largest selection of teas, coffees and hot chocolates on offer under one roof! There's soya milk available too so no need for vegans to miss out on a smoothie or the 30 hot chocolate options.
Hot Chocolate £2.20, Ice Tea £2, Milkshake £2.20, Smoothies £2.30-2.50, Cakes £2.20
Opening Hours: Sunday - Monday 8am - 6pm
Saturday 8am - 6pm

Donatello (Pizzeria Ristorante)

1-3 Brighton Place, Brighton BN1 1HJ
Tel: 01273 775477
E: donatellobrighton@compuserve.com
W: www.donatello.co.uk

Type of Cuisine: Italian
Breakdown: (out of 46 dishes) Vegetarian: 20%; Vegan: 5%
This very popular Italian is right in the heart of the Lanes. It's a genuine family run restaurant priding itself on its hospitality. You can dine inside or outside and there's plenty of vegetarian options.

Melanzane alla Parmigiana (aubergines baked with tomato, mozzarella, bechamel & parmesan cheese) £4.90, Spaghetti (gluten free or wholewheat also available) Aglio Olio e Peperoncino (olive oil, garlic, chilli & parsley) £5.35, Tagliatelle alla Siciliana (aubergine, green peppers, garlic, olives, capers, tomato & parsley) £6
Opening Hours: Every day 11.30am - 11.30pm

Food For Friends (Restaurant) ✔ 10%

17-18 Prince Albert Street, Brighton BN1 1HF
Tel: 01273 202310
W: www.foodforfriends.com
Type of Cuisine: Global Vegetarian
Breakdown: (out of 10 dishes) Vegetarian: 100%; Vegan: 20%
Food for Friends is a very popular café and restaurant. It has moved with the times, from its lentilly beginning in 1981 to a fresh and modern place to be. They now serve imaginative dishes from seasonal ingredients, sourced from local Sussex producers which are all GMO-free and organic where possible. The portions are generous and the salads are a tempting healthy treat in the summer. Wash it all down with organic beers and wines which are all vegan, or a fruit smoothie, or even a cocktail. In the evening, Food For Friends transforms from a busy cafe to a romantic restaurant with pine tables, candles and fresh flowers.
Cauliflower & Dill Soup £3.50, Plum & Sesame Tofu with Ginger Bok Choi (V) £3.90, Warm Mediterranean Vegetable Crostoni with Caper & Basil Drizzle (V) £8.95
Opening Hours: Monday - Saturday 8am - 10pm
Sunday 9.15am - 10pm

Gars (Restaurant)

19 Prince Albert Street, Brighton BN1 1HF
Tel: 01273 321321
E: garsrestaurant@tiscali.co.uk

Type of Cuisine: Chinese
Breakdown: (out of 70 dishes) Vegetarian: 25%; Vegan: 20%
This sleek, stylish red and silver restaurant is perfect for parties of 10 or more; with a large booth to cater for you and plenty of vegetarian options to choose from. The Monk's Feast (£21.50) is their vegetarian set menu and is a tasty whirlwind of flavours. Children (up to seven years old) are welcome until 7pm.

Skewered Vegetable Satay £5.50, Tempura Aubergines or Sweet Potatoes with Dip £6, Hot & Sour Soup £4.50, Pak Choi Stir-fried Toban Style (spicy, chilli & garlic) £7, Bean Curd in Ginger & Spring Onions £8.50
Opening Hours: Monday - Sunday noon - 11pm

The Hop Poles (Pub)

13 Middle Street, Brighton BN1 1AL
Tel: 01273 710444

Type of Cuisine: Global
Breakdown: (out of 19 dishes) Vegetarian: 50%; Vegan: 10%
Popular pub, good vibes, friendly staff and tasty veggie options – a winning combination. The stripped pine floors and furniture give the place a fresh feel and the patio garden is well designed. It gets really packed so arrive early for a table. Three chefs cook for the menu which changes daily.

Nut Terrine Platter (with chips, avocado basil, feta & tomato salad, potato salad & pasta salad) £4, Channa Sag Aloo (great veggie curry) £4, Three Cheese Stuffed Mushrooms £4, Brie & Cranberry Super Sandwich £2.95

Opening Hours: Sunday - Thursday noon - 9pm
Friday & Saturday noon - 8pm

The King and I (Restaurant)

2 Ship Street, Brighton BN1 1AD
Tel: 01273 773390

Type of Cuisine: Thai
Breakdown: (out of 80 dishes) Vegetarian: 30%; Vegan: 20%
Two floors of classy comfortable seating to relax in while you enjoy the subtle delights of Thai food. Top quality cuisine delicately cooked and beautifully presented. Dark and woody, this place is ideal for a romantic meal. Booking is advisable as it's deservedly very popular.
Tod Man Kao Pood (deep fried sweetcorn with a sweet sauce) £4.15, Masamanja (bean curd in a curry sauce with potatoes & peanuts) £5.55, Hed Himmiphan (fried mushrooms with cashew nuts & chilli) £5.50
Opening Hours: Monday 6pm - 11pm
Tuesday - Thursday 12.30pm - 3pm & 6pm - 11pm
Friday - Sunday 12.30pm - 3pm & 6pm - 11.30pm

Krakatoa (Restaurant)

7 Pool Valley, Brighton BN1 1NJ
Tel: 01273 719009
E: krakatoa_brighton@yahoo.com
W: www.krakatoa.fsnet.co.uk

Type of Cuisine: Modern Oriental Vegetarian and Seafood
Breakdown: (out of 30 dishes) Vegetarian: 50%; Vegan: 20%
Beautifully prepared, tasty oriental morsels! The simple pine furniture, terracotta walls and plants make for an exquisite dining experience. Upstairs is a real treat – you get to sit on cushions on the floor – it really does make the food taste

even more authentic!

Thai Noodles, Tofu & Beansprouts £7.50, Gado Gado (vegetables, potatoes, tofu & tempeh in a spicy peanut sauce) £8.50, Massaman Curry £8.50, Lumpia (Indonesian spring rolls with sweet chilli sauce) £4.75

Opening Hours: Every day 6pm - 11pm

Lanes Deli & Pasta Shop

12b Meeting House Lane, Brighton BN1 1HB
Tel: 01273 723522

Type of Cuisine: Pasta, Pizza Slices, Breads
Breakdown: (out of 15 dishes) Vegetarian: 40%; Vegan: 10%
Great for an unusual take-away lunch of fresh pasta (made with eggs) and home-made sauce. There are gluten-free sauces available and at least half of the sauces are veggie. Also pizza slices, focaccia and ciabatta sandwiches, olives, Belgian chocolates and tiramisu – yum!
Take-away Pasta 'n' Sauce (choose from up to 10) £2.50
Opening Hours: Monday - Saturday 10am - 6.30pm
Sunday 11.30am - 5pm

Moshi Moshi (Sushi Bar)

Bartholomew Square, Brighton BN1 1JF
Tel: 01273 719195

Type of Cuisine: Sushi
Breakdown: (out of 45 dishes) Vegetarian: 10%; Vegan: 10%
Chic and modern, this conveyor belt sushi bar is good fun and a great treat, offering veggie fast food as it should be – completely nutritious and tasty. The building is really unusual, made from translucent material so it looks like a large lantern hovering over the square. Watch out for the Wasabi (hot horseradish style green paste) – it's really hot!

My mum thought it was an avocado dip and spent our meal with steam coming out of her ears and glugging as much water as we could get our hands on.

Vegetarian Sushi Pack (and exciting range of vegetarian Maki) £5.50 (take out), Vegetarian Selection £5.90 (eat in), Vegetarian Bento Box with Spicy Tofu Omlette £14.50 (take out)

Opening Hours: Sunday - Thursday noon - 10pm
Friday & Saturday noon - 11pm

Old Orleans (Restaurant)

1-3 Prince Albert Street, Brighton BN1 1HE
Tel: 01273 747000

Type of Cuisine: American

Breakdown: (out of 100 dishes) Vegetarian: 20%; Vegan: 0%

Old Orleans invites you to enjoy their Southern hospitality, a veggie burger and a cocktail to wash it down – hic!

Vegetable Jambalaya £8.75, Veggie Fajitas £9.95, Jalapeno Peppers £4.75

Opening Hours: Every day noon - 11pm

The Opposition Café (Take-Away)

41 Market Street, Brighton BN1 1HH
Tel: 01273 748801

Type of Cuisine: Sandwiches and Cakes

Breakdown: (out of 60 dishes) Vegetarian: 10%; Vegan: 5%

Classy, clean and groovy, The Opposition caters for the modern muncher. Basically, choose your ideal filling combination and have the sandwich of your dreams.

Panini Bread with Brie & Roasted Vegetables £4.50 (eat in)/£3.80 (take out), Jacket Potato (various fillings) £3 - £6, Chocolate Cake, Carrot Cake, Cheesecake £1.50 - £3.50

Opening Hours: Every day 7am - midnight

Piccolos (Restaurant)   **V** 10%

56 Ship Street, Brighton BN1 1AF
Tel: 01273 380380

Type of Cuisine: Italian
Breakdown: (out of 40 dishes) Vegetarian: 50%; Vegan: 10%
A bustling, very popular restaurant offering exceptionally good value. The food is prepared to order and the chef promises to be flexible. So just let them know your requirements and they will feed you. There's a few tasty vegan treats and even a take-away pizza service.
Margarita Pizza £3.60, Ravioli Bosciola £5.50, Spaghetti Napoletana (V) £4.30
Opening Hours: Every day 11.30am - 11.30pm

Pizza Express (Restaurant)

22 Prince Albert Street, Brighton BN1 1HF
Tel: 01273 323205

Type of Cuisine: Italian Pizza
Breakdown: (out of 20 dishes) Vegetarian: 40%; Vegan: 15%
Popular franchise with chic black and white décor. The pizzas are delicious. If you're vegan don't be put off – just say no to the cheese.
Gardinia £6.65, Venziana (ask for no cheese) (V) £4.75
Opening Hours: Every day 11.30am - midnight

The Prodigal (Pub/Restaurant)

80 East Street, Brighton BN1 1NF
Tel: 01273 748103

Type of Cuisine: Global
Breakdown: (out of 30 dishes) Vegetarian: 30%; Vegan: 10%
A large pub which gets packed out on Friday and Saturday nights. It's on the corner of East Street and the sea front so

*it's got great views and is an easy option if you've been
sunning yourself on the beach or swimming between the
piers and need sustenance! The food is reasonably priced for
the generous portions and there's something on the menu
for everyone, whether you're feeling like a healthy salad or
burger and fries.*

Veggie Bangers & Mash £4.95, Home-made Chilli Veggie
Burger with Fries & Salad £4.85, Hummus & Roasted
Vegetable Wrap with Tortilla Chips £4.85, Nacho Mountain
with Vegetable Chilli £5.95

Opening Hours: Monday, Tuesday & Thursday - Saturday
noon - 9pm Wednesday noon - 6pm Sunday noon - 5pm

Santa Fe (Bar/Grill)

75-79 East Street, Brighton BN1 1NF
Tel: 01273 823231
E: brightonsf@santafe.co.uk

Type of Cuisine: Grilled!

Breakdown: (out of 30 dishes) Vegetarian: 20%; Vegan: 10%
*This is an impressive venue with a bar area that looks like it
should be in a film. The décor is rich and warm with dark
wood and deep orange paint work. You can watch your
food being cooked in the grill area upstairs.*

Ricotta & Spinach Crepes £7.25, Aubergine Parmigiana £7.95,
Corn Tortilla Chips & Dips £3.95, Warm Greek Salad £4.25
(small) or £7.95 (large)

Opening Hours: Every day noon - 10.30pm

The Strand (Restaurant)

6 Little East Street, Brighton BN1 1HT
Tel: 01273 747096

Type of Cuisine: Global

Breakdown: (out of 35 dishes) Vegetarian: 30%; Vegan: 5%

The Strand is cosy, marine and special, the wooden furniture gives the place a really nice feel – I like to sit upstairs and overlook the street below. They have quality food put together in imaginative ways, so if you fancy something a bit different this is the place. The vegan choice is limited but as the food is all freshly prepared, the friendly staff are willing to adapt a dish to suit your needs.

Chestnut, Sweet Onion, Mushroom & Cranberry Steamed Roly-poly on Mashed Potato with Rich Port Wine Gravy £13.25, Melting Camembert, Aubergine & Sun-dried Tomato Tarte Tatin Resting on a Crispy Onion Fritter £12.95

Opening Hours: Tuesday - Thursday 12.30pm - 10pm
Saturday & Sunday 12.30pm - 10.30pm
Sunday 6pm - 10pm

Terre à Terre (Restaurant)

71 East Street, Brighton BN1 1HQ
Tel: 01273 729051
W: www.terreaterre.co.uk

Type of Cuisine: Global Vegetarian

Breakdown: (out of 30 dishes) Vegetarian: 100%; Vegan: 50%

Recently voted No 2 restaurant in the UK by the readers of the Observer Food Monthly magazine, Terre à Terre is renowned for its innovative and delicious cuisine. The food is a fusion of worldwide influences; it's a bit like someone's been experimenting with foods and flavours and got it so right every time. The chefs make an effort to source organic and local ingredients and really care about the food they serve. It's always beautifully presented and even though you probably won't understand the lavish descriptions on the menu, each dish is destined to delight your taste buds. The

Vegan Terre à Tapas is a firm Viva! favourite. The décor is rich purples and warm oranges, it is natural and spacious. Early booking is necessary for evening meals but not lunch.
Wasabi Cashews £2.90, Beanshoot Fritters (served with capiscum shred & black bean tamari glaze) £4.95, Parmesan Dunk Doughnuts (parmesan doughnut stuffed with shallot compot & cranberry cippolini, rolled in bark spice salt, with hot chestnut cheese duk & macey milk bay cream) £5, Terre à Tapas – good to share (vegan option) (a selection of lovelies, hot & cold, served with garlic & herb focaccia) £14.50, Meady Meadow Mulled Barrel (vegan option) (leeks barrels rammed full of marrow beans, chunked garlic caramel & English parsley mash, with sage butter & fried bread sauce barberry dumplings) £12.50
Opening Hours: Tuesday 6.30pm - 10.30pm
Wednesday - Friday noon - 3pm & 6.30pm - 10.30pm
Saturday noon - 11pm Sunday noon - 10.30pm

Kemptown, Hove & Beyond Town Kemptown

Alice's (Café)

113 St George's Road, Brighton BN2 1EA
Tel: 01273 691790

Type of Cuisine: Coffee Shop and Take-Away
Breakdown: (out of 50 dishes) Vegetarian: 30%; Vegan: 0%
This Kemptown café is one of the most popular in the area –
probably because it has lots of choices on the menu and the
staff are friendly. The veggie selection is quite basic – jacket
potatoes, macaroni cheese and such like, but good snacks.
Veggie Breakfast (veggie sausage, egg, mushrooms, beans,
tomatoes & hash browns) £4.50, Eggs, Beans & Chips £2.50,
Welsh Rarebit £2.50, Mushrooms on Toast £1.90, Hot
Chocolate with Whipped Cream £1.65
Opening Hours: Monday - Saturday 9am - 4pm
Sunday closed

The Barley Mow (Pub)

92 St George's Road, Brighton BN2 1EE
Tel: 01273 682259

Type of Cuisine: Pub Food
Breakdown: (out or 40 dishes) Vegetarian: 25%; Vegan: 10%
Here you'll find a warm welcome, an outside eating area and
fab décor – you might just want to move in! With warning
they will try to accommodate vegans and any allergies. They
offer a good vegetarian selection and big portions.
Home-made Veggie Burger, Chips & Salad £6.95, Veggie
Sausage, Pesto Mash & Red Wine Gravy £5.95, Veggie Fajitas,

Chips & Salad £5.95, and on Sundays Nut Roast £6.50, Posh Pie £6.50 or Chestnut Wellington £6.95 followed by Chocolate Fudge Cake £2.75

Opening Hours: Monday - Saturday 11am - 10pm
Sunday noon - 10pm

Brighton Rocks (Restaurant/Bar)

6 Rock Place, Brighton BN2 1PF
Tel: 01273 601139

Type of Cuisine: Modern Global
Breakdown: (out of 15 dishes) Vegetarian: 40%; Vegan: 20%
This place has undergone an extreme make-over, from an old stuffy pub to a chic, modern cocktail bar with an 80% organic menu. The chef is very enthusiastic and experimental, as shown in the menu.
Buffalo Mozzarella, Beef Tomato, Rocket, Green & Purple Basil, Roasted Pine Nuts, Reduced Balsamic Dressing & Parmesan Swirls £7.50, Honey Roasted Butternut Squash, Toasted Walnuts, Fresh Figs, Whole Roasted Baby Shallots & Herb Salad (can be made vegan) £7.50, Poached Pears in Ginger Wine & Saffron £4.50
Opening Hours: Monday - Friday noon - 8pm
Saturday & Sunday noon - 5pm

Café Bohemia

57 St James' Street, Brighton BN2 1QG
Tel: 01273 609832

Type of Cuisine: Breakfasts and Hot Snacks
Breakdown: (out of 30 dishes) Vegetarian: 10%; Vegan: 0%
Café Bohemia is the place for the hungry veggie – check out the mega veggie breakfast if you want to fuel up.
Mega Veggie Breakfast £4.95, Regular Veggie Breakfast

£2.60, Chips & Beans (V) £1.30, Veggie Burger & Chips £2.75, Jacket Potatoes from £1.20
Opening Hours: Every day 8am - 6pm

The Dragon (Pub)

St George's Road, Kemptown BN2 1EF
Tel: 01273 690144

Type of Cuisine: Various
Breakdown: (out of 17 dishes) Vegetarian: 20%; Vegan: 5%
A funky and friendly pub with a Jamaican menu. The pub feels cosy and comfortable with dragon images everywhere. The veggie options are reasonably priced and the portions are generous.
Veggie Taco £3, Fried Plantain £2.50, ITAL (veggie dahl, aubergine, garlic, potatoes & salad) £5
Opening Hours: Monday - Thursday noon - 11pm Friday & Saturday noon - midnight Sunday noon - 10.30pm

La Capannina (Ristorante/Pizzeria Italiano)

15 Madeira Place, Brighton BN2 1TN
Tel: 01273 680839

Type of Cuisine: Italian
Breakdown: (out of 100 dishes) Vegetarian: 25%; Vegan: 5%
La Capannina is renowned as one of the best Italians in Brighton and has a large vegetarian selection. Just off the sea front, La Capannina is cosy and has an authentic Italian feel.
Rigatoni Siciliana (Rigatoni with aubergines, garlic & tomato, baked with mozzarella cheese) £7.20, Penne Fiorentina (Penne with spinach, tomato, basil & mozzarella) £6.95, Gnocchi Ripieni Di Ricotta E Spinaci (fresh potato dumplings filled with ricotta cheese & spinach with a creamy tomato sauce) £7.95, Pizza Alla Rucola (rocket, parmesan & pecorino cheese) £6.95

Opening Hours: Monday - Saturday noon - 2.30pm &
6pm - 11.30pm Sunday 6pm - 11.30pm

Market Diner (Café)

19-21 Circus Street, Brighton BN2 9QF
Tel: 01273 608273

Type of Cuisine: Fast Food
Breakdown: (out of 30 dishes) Vegetarian: 20%; Vegan: 0%
*This is the place to go if you happen to be either a market
trader or an insomniac. Yes, it's open all night so beat those
midnight munchies, head for the Market Diner and treat
yourself to an all night breakfast. They can do a vegan
version if you ask them nicely.*

Vegi-Buster (just about everything you can think of in a
greasy spoon) £3.40
Opening Hours: Sunday - Friday 9.30pm -11am
Saturday 9.30pm - 9am Sunday 9.30pm - 6am

Muang Thai (Restaurant)

77 St James' Street, Brighton BN2 1PA
Tel: 01273 605223

Type of Cuisine: Thai
Breakdown: (out of 100 dishes) Vegetarian: 20%; Vegan: 10%
*The décor is sparse and stylish, and the food is rich and tasty.
I recommend the vegetarian set menu which can be made
vegan and is like a journey through the flavours and textures
of Thailand.*

Vegetarian Set Menu – Sa-Tay Hed (mushrooms with peanut
sauce), Mim Thai Spring Rolls, Fried Mung Bean Noodles, Fried
Bean Curd, Red Curry & Rice with a dessert to complete £12.95
Opening Hours: Every day 12.30pm - 3pm & 6.30pm - midnight

Nasim Pizza (Take-Away)

100 St James' Street, Brighton BN2 1TP
Tel: 01273 606303

Type of Cuisine: Pizza, Sandwiches and Jacket Potatoes
Breakdown: (out of 50 dishes) Vegetarian: 40%; Vegan: 5%
I often get a whiff of hot pizza as I dash past Nasim Pizza on my way home and it smells great. They bake their own bread and the pizzas are freshly prepared with a choice of 12 veggie toppings. There's also loads of toppings and fillings for baguettes and jacket potatoes.
Amigo Pizza (tomato, cheese, mushroom, onion, garlic, sweetcorn & peppers) £2.70/£3.70, Mamma Mia Pizza (tomato, cheese, mushroom, chilli powder, garlic, mixed herbs, banana & pinapple) £2.70/£3.70, Tutti Fruitty Pizza (tomato, cheese, pinapple, banana & curry) £2.70/£3.70, Veggie Salad Box £3, Vegetable Lasagne £2.55, Samosa £1.20, Potato Cake £1.20, Cheese & Onion Pasty £1.50
Opening Hours: Every day 8.30am - late

Saint James (Pub)

16 Madeira Place, Brighton BN2 1TN
Tel: 01273 626696

Type of Cuisine: Various
Breakdown: (out of 11 dishes) Vegetarian: 40%; Vegan: 0%
Popular pub with a few veggie delights on offer. Don't forget to check out the specials board.
Home-made Hummus with Cucumber & Olive Salad & Hot Pitta £3.50, Mushroom, Brie & Avocado Melt £3.95
Opening Hours: Monday - Saturday 12.30pm - 6pm
Sunday 1pm - 6pm

The Sidewinder (Pub)

65 Upper St James' Street, Brighton BN2 1JN
Tel: 01273 679927

Type of Cuisine: Various
Breakdown: (out of 30 dishes) Vegetarian: 20%; Vegan: 10%
If you're heading into town from Kemptown you'll spot this pub by the giant crab painted on the side of the building. The Sidewinder offers a funky, relaxed atmosphere and tasty food. The wood floors, chunky tables and sofas encourage you to stay all day and the large garden is ideal for sunny days.
Pasta with Spinach, Pine Nuts & Garlic Sauce £5.95, Deli Wrap with Feta, Pine Nuts, Tomato & Pesto £3.95, Deli Wrap with Grilled Squash, Peppers & Rocket £3.95, Deli Wrap with Spinach Feta & Roasted Peppers £5.95, Wild Mushroom Burger £5.95
Opening Hours: Every day 6pm - 10.30pm

The Street Coffee Shop (Café)

101 St James' Street, Brighton BN2 1TP
Tel: 01273 673891

Type of Cuisine: Breakfasts, Burgers, Sandwiches and Cakes
Breakdown: (out of 80 dishes) Vegetarian: 25%; Vegan: 15%
This café is fresh and cool. Their big bonus is the back garden – a leafy, homely place to hang out on a hot summer afternoon. Soya milk is always available and their sausages are vegan. Local magazine G-Scene has given them the title of best veggie breakfast in Brighton for the last two years.
Veggie Pasta (V) £4.55, Veggie Wrap £4.25, Veggie Breakfast £3.95, Veggie Pizza £4.55, Spicy Bean Burger £4.75
Opening Hours: Monday - Saturday 10am - 5.30pm

The Tin Drum (Bar/Restaurant)

43 St James' Street, Brighton BN2 1RG
Tel: 01273 624777
& 95-97 Dyke Road, Brighton BN1 3JE
Tel: 01273 777575
& 10 Victoria Grove, Second Avenue, Hove BN3 2LG
Tel: 01273 747755
E: tindrum@tindrum.co.uk

Type of Cuisine: Global Creations!

Breakdown: (out of 36 dishes) Vegetarian: 20%; Vegan: 10%

I highly recommend the Tin Drum, the atmosphere is great, the staff are really friendly and the food is top quality. The stylish bar (sells cocktails and good wine) and restaurant is proving popular in Kemptown following the success of the Seven Dials Tin Drum. If you're vegan just tell them and they'll create something for you. The food is locally sourced where possible and they try not to use any GM foods.

Vegetarian Burger £7.95, Italian Vegetables & Cannelini Bean Casserole £7.95, Tomato, Gruyere & Shallot Melt £4.95

Opening Hours: Saturday & Sunday 10am - 5pm & 6pm - 10pm
Friday 11am - 5pm & 6pm - 10pm
Monday - Thursday 11am - 2.30pm & 6pm - 9.30pm

Hove

Ashoka (Restaurant)

95-97 Church Road, Hove BN3 2BA
Tel: 01273 734193

Type of Cuisine: Indian/English
Breakdown: (out of 100 dishes) Vegetarian: 25%; Vegan: 5%
A truly authentic tandoori restaurant. The blend of Indian food and music make for a spicy sensory experience. The choice of vegetarian dishes is limited but high quality, so if you're the indecisive type then this one could be for you. Not much on offer for vegans – a few side dishes perhaps.
Vegetable Biriani £5.55, Mixed Vegetable Rogan £3.95, Garlic Naan £1.75, Sunday Buffet (noon-3pm) £6.95 (adult) £3.95 (under 14s)
Opening Hours: Every day noon - 3pm & 6pm - midnight

Bali Brasserie (Restaurant)

Kingsway Court, First Avenue, Hove BN3 2LR
Tel: 01273 323810

Type of Cuisine: Indonesian/Malaysian
Breakdown: (out of 50 dishes) Vegetarian: 15%; Vegan: 10%
Large restaurant, ideal for big parties, with lots of veggie and vegan options to choose from.
Aubergines, Courgettes & Potatoes in a Coconut, Lemon Grass & Lime Leaf Sauce £2.45, Stir-fry Beansprouts in a Spicy Pepper Sauce £2.45, Potatoes & Chickpeas in a Mild Curry Sauce £2.45
Opening Hours: Sunday - Thursday 12.30pm - 2pm & 6.30pm - 10.30pm
Friday & Saturday 12.30pm - 2pm & 6.30pm - 11pm

The Fortune Cookie (Take-Away)

35 Boundary Road, Hove BN3 4EF
Tel: 01273 418860

Type of Cuisine: Chinese
Breakdown: (out of 123 dishes) Vegetarian: 7%; Vegan: 6%
The Fortune Cookie specialises in Szechuan, Cantonese and Peking cuisine and are willing to cook what your heart desires and deliver it to your door. The range of vegetarian and vegan delicacies is limited compared to the amount of meat dishes they do. However look closely at the back page of the menu and you will find a few things to delight you.
Vegetarian Spring Roll £1.50, Mixed Vegetable Chow Mein £3, Fried Mixed Vegetables with Cashew Nuts in Fermented Soya Bean Sauce £3.10, Sweet & Sour Mixed Vegetables £2.80, Mushroom Foo Yung £3
Opening Hours: Monday, Wednesday & Thursday noon - 2pm & 5pm - 11.30pm
Friday & Saturday noon - 2pm & 5pm - midnight
Sunday 5pm - 11.30pm

Halangers Restaurant

14 Blatchington Road, Hove BN3 3YN
Tel: 01273 205009

Type of Cuisine: Various
Breakdown: (out of 10 dishes) Vegetarian: 20%; Vegan: 5%
Relaxed, intimate and friendly with imaginative and freshly cooked food. On three levels and seating just 22-24 people, Halangers is ideal for that romantic meal for two. The menu changes fortnightly and it's best to let them know if you're vegan before you go. Most of the starters are vegetarian and there's always at least one veggie option on the main menu.
Red Lentil, Carrot & Tomato Soup (V), Bulghur & Winter

Vegetable Loaf with a Red Currant & Red Wine Sauce, Spring Roll with Exotic Vegetables in a Sweet & Sour Sauce on a Bed of Wild Rice £14.50 for two courses, £17 for three courses
Opening Hours: Sunday & Tuesday closed
Other days 11.30am - 1.30pm & 6.30pm - 9.30pm

Ipanema (Restaurant)

121 Western Road, Hove BN3 1DB
Tel: 01273 779474
W: www.ipanemarestaurants.com
Type of Cuisine: Greek and Spanish
Breakdown: (out of 200 dishes) Vegetarian: 10%; Vegan: 0%
Ipanema says: 'When you're in a Mediterranean country on holiday the food tastes great. It's not just the flavours, it's the atmosphere and you can find these at Ipanema restaurant in Hove.' The food is freshly prepared and it's based on traditional home-made recipes from Greece and Spain.
Cannelloni Florentina £4.90, Rigatoni Primavera with Vegetable, Cream & White Wine £4.50, Vegetarian Stuffed Peppers £6.20, Patatas Bravas (deep-fried potatoes in a spicy sauce) £2.70
Opening Hours: Monday - Friday 10.30am - midnight
Saturday & Sunday 11am - midnight

Jasmine (Take-Away)

238 Portland Road, Brighton BN3 5QT
Tel: 01273 723830
Type of Cuisine: Chinese
Breakdown: (out of 100 dishes) Vegetarian: 30%; Vegan: 25%
The vegetarian section on the menu is great, there's loads to choose from and there's a delivery service too.
Garlic Mushrooms £3.60, Satay Tofu on Skewer £4, Szechuan

Aubergine £4, Peking Grill Tofu with Garlic & Ginger Sauce
£4, Sweet & Sour Mixed Vegetables £3.60
Opening Hours: Monday - Sunday 5pm - 11pm

Oki-Nami (Restaurant)

208 Church Road, Hove BN3 2DJ
Tel: 01273 773777

Type of Cuisine: Japanese
Breakdown: (out of 98 dishes) Vegetarian: 28%; Vegan: 20%
*Oki-Nami caters for veggies and vegans with a creative menu
and some unusual vegan dishes at very reasonable prices.*
Sushi with mushroom or pickled plum £3, Hijiki (seaweed,
noodles & vegetables) £2.95, Horenso (spinach in seasame
sauce) £3, Age Tofu £2.95
Opening Hours: Every day noon - 2.30pm & 6pm - 10.30pm
Tuesday lunchtime closed

Papadoms Indian (Restaurant)

75 Portland Road, Hove BN3 5DP
Tel: 01273 729602

Type of Cuisine: Indian
Breakdown: (out of 70 dishes) Vegetarian: 25%; Vegan: 25%
*Eat in, take-away or have your meal delivered – it's all the
same price. There are 20 vegetarian dishes to choose from
and they're all priced between £1.95 and £2.95 so order a
few to share.*
Vegetable Bhuna £2.95, Vegetarian Soup £1.45, Vegetable
Jalfry £2.95, Dahl £2.75, Sag Aloo £2.95, Bhindi Bhaji £2.95
Opening Hours: Sunday - Thursday noon - 2pm & 5.30pm - 11.30pm
Friday & Saturday noon - 2pm & 5.30pm - midnight

The Sanctuary (Café/Bar)

51-55 Brunswick Street East, Hove BN3 1AU
Tel: 01273 770002
W: www.sanctuarycafe.co.uk

Type of Cuisine: Global

Breakdown: (out of 40 dishes) Vegetarian: 95%; Vegan: 30%
The Sanctuary is totally groovy. The sassy lime greens,
oranges and blues that surround you while you lounge on
the sofa upstairs supping cappuccino can make even the
most geeky of people feel totally with it – I know! The
blackboard has five main dishes which change daily and the
standard is consistently high. There's usually at least one
vegan option on there and the soup is always vegan. The
Sanctuary is mostly vegetarian but serves fish too.
Moroccan Vegetable Stew with Basmati Rice (V) £5.25,
Spinach & Thai Spice Soup with Bread (V) £2.45, Vegetables
Sautéed in Coconut, Chilli, Coriander & Brandy £5.25

Opening Hours: Monday noon - 11.30pm
Tuesday - Sunday 10am - 11.30pm

Saucy (Restaurant)

8 Church Road, Hove BN3 2FL
Tel: 01273 324080

Type of Cuisine: British

Breakdown: (out of 17 dishes) Vegetarian: 35%; Vegan: 0%
The food is British in essence but includes influences from
many cultures and the menu changes monthly to keep up
with what's in season. The emphasis here is on enjoyment –
the staff are friendly and the décor is beautiful and stylish.
Red Onion Tarte Tatin (caramelised red onions on a puff
pastry base, topped with marinated feta cheese & garnished
with a dressed rocket & roast tomato salad) £4.75, Roasted

Pumpkin Squash (filled with an apricot, mushroom & sage wild rice stuffing & finished with a cardamon sauce) £8.95, Spinach & Mushroom Roulade £8.75
Opening Hours: Monday - Friday noon - 3pm & 6pm - 10.30pm Saturday & Sunday noon - late

The Spanish Connection (Restaurant)

38 Waterloo Street, Hove BN3 1AY
Tel: 01273 747555
E: tapashouse@aol.com
Type of Cuisine: Spanish Tapas
Breakdown: (out of 30 dishes) Vegetarian: 35%; Vegan: 33%
Spanish Connection offers a selection of 11 vegetarian dishes plus daily specials. If you want something a bit different come here and experience a bit of Spain, even if it's cold and raining in Brighton!
Patatas Bravas £2.50 or Tortilla Espanola £2.50, Garbanzos Con Espinacas (V) £2.75, Pisto (stewed summer vegetables) £2.95, Berenjenas Fritas (deep-fried battered aubergine) £2.75
Opening Hours: Tuesday - Saturday 7pm - late

Beyond the Town Centre

The Bear (Pub)

Lewes Road, Brighton BN2 4AE
Tel: 01273 672233

Type of Cuisine: Classic Pub Food
Breakdown: (out of 30 dishes) Vegetarian: 15%; Vegan: 0%
Cosy and friendly, this classic pub is decked out in dark wood and popular with students, possibly due to it's closeness to some of the university buildings and the value-for-money-menu. The walls are busily decorated with interesting pictures, games and crockery.
Crunchy Mushrooms (breaded mushrooms with garlic mayonnaise & a generous side salad) £2.25, Jacket Potato with Coleslaw & Cheese £2.50
Opening Hours (food): Every day noon - 3pm

The Cowley Club (Café)

12 London Road, Brighton BN1 4JA
Tel: 01273 696104

Type of Cuisine: Café
Breakdown: (out of 30 dishes) Vegetarian 100%; Vegan: 90%
Run by a team of volunteers this is a great place to get a meal at great value. There's plenty of reading material too; from the history of anarchy to biodynamic vegetable growing, there's something for everyone!
Soup of the Day (V) £1.50, Jacket Potato with Hummus/Chilli/Beans (V) £1.50, Tortilla Wraps (V) £1.70, Selection of Vegan Cakes 50p
Opening Hours: Tuesday - Friday noon - 4pm Thursday noon - 7pm

The Dover Castle (Pub)

43 Southover Street, Brighton BN2 9UE
Tel: 01273 688276

Type of Cuisine: Global
Breakdown: (out of 12 dishes) Vegetarian: 95%; Vegan: 50%
Well prepared, tasty, unusual vegetarian and vegan food at really reasonable prices – well worth the trek up the hill! As well as the normal veggie menu, there's a specials board and on Sundays check out the Caribbean-style roast dinner. The only non-veggie dish is one of the Sunday roasts. If you fancy a pint while you're waiting for your food, be assured that all the draught lagers are vegan – hoorah!
Sombrero Baguette (spicy chirozo sausage & salsa in a baguette served with an olive salad) (V) £3.70, Thai Corn Cakes (spicy sweetcorn fritters on a bed of lime & coriander rice, served with garlic & chilli sauce) (V) £4.20, Lemon & Rosemary Pasta Penne (durum wheat pasta bound in a home-made walnut pesto) £4.10
Opening Hours: Monday - Friday noon - 3pm & 5pm - 8pm (food) Saturday noon - 5pm & Sunday from 1pm

Shada Thai Cuisine (Restaurant)

4 Lewes Road, Brighton BN2 3HP
Tel: 01273 677608

Type of Cuisine: Thai
Breakdown: (out of 69 dishes) Vegetarian: 50%; Vegan: 5%
Shada offer an extensive and truly delicious range of sauces – sweet & sour, black bean, yellow curry and many more – as basic dishes which you can choose to have with tofu and vegetables. Although the Lewes Road location is quite grim, inside this restaurant it is rich and colourful. Let your karma be purified while you wallow in the presence of Buddha

images and soft candle light.
Yellow Curry with Tofu £6.50, Shada Pad Roum with Spicy
Mixed Vegetables Wok-fried in Spicy Sauce £4.99, Pad Thai
Noodles £6.50
Opening Hours: Tuesday - Saturday 6pm - 11pm
Sunday 6pm - 10pm

The Tin Drum (Bar/Restaurant)

95-97 Dyke Road, Brighton BN1 3JE
Tel: 01273 777575
E: tindrum@tindrum.co.uk
Also in Kemptown (see page 80)

Lewes

The Garden Room (Café)

14 Station Street, Lewes BN7 2DA
Tel: 01273 478636

Type of Cuisine: Cakes and Snacks
Breakdown: (out of 18 dishes) Vegetarian: 95%; Vegan: 10%
The Garden Room is available for party bookings in the evenings (minimum number six) and they have regular exhibitions of paintings. They serve cream teas and a range of home-made cakes as well as many tasty vegetarian dishes.
Nut Loaf with Apricot Sauce £3.80, Spinach & Mushroom Roulade £3.80, Savoury Pancake Gateaux £3.80, Jacket Potatoes with Various Fillings £4.20
Opening Hours: Monday - Saturday 10am - 5.30pm

Seasons of Lewes (Café)

199 High Street, Lewes BN7 2NS
Tel: 01273 473968

Type of Cuisine: Vegetarian
Breakdown: (out of 7 dishes) Vegetarian: 100%; Vegan: 60%
Refreshing to see a café so committed to vegetarianism, organic produce and value for money. Their slogan is 'Seasons – Food For People Who Care About What They Eat' and this mother and daughter team obviously care about what they cook.
Organic Pumpkin & Ginger Soup with Wholemeal Bread (V) £2.75, Brazil & Cashew Roast with Tomato & Herb Sauce (V) £4, Butterbean & Cider Casserole with Organic Brown Rice (V) £4, Leek & Mushroom Pie (V) £4, Organic Carrot Cake £1.50
Opening Hours: Tuesday - Saturday 9.30am - 5.30pm

Shanaz Tandoori & Balti Restaurant

83 High Street, Lewes BN7 1XN
Tel: 01273 488028

Type of Cuisine: Indian
Breakdown: (out of 30 dishes) Vegetarian: 25%; Vegan: 5%
*Spice up your life at Shanaz! They adapt their specialities
for vegetarians.*
Indian Garlic Mushrooms £2.90, Vegetable Samosa £2.50,
Vegetable-stuffed Naan £1.50, Aloo Gobi £3.25, Tarka Dahl £3.25
Opening Hours: Every day noon - 2.30pm & 6pm - 12.30am

The Snowdrop (Pub)

119 South Street, Lewes BN7 2BU
Tel: 01273 471018

Type of Cuisine: Global
Breakdown: (out of 50 dishes) Vegetarian: 90%; Vegan: 50%
*A personal favourite! Great atmosphere with loads of
character and odd bits of everything old and arty decorating
the walls and every available corner. There's really fab food –
including vegan pizza and the Sunday roast is generous and
tasty too. The vegan options are clearly marked with stars on
the menu and labelled on the specials board. They use organic
ingredients wherever possible and the food is all GM-free.*
Garlic Mushrooms (V) £3.50, Vege Burger (V) £2.60, Brie &
Black Grape Sandwich £2, Erbivoro Pizza (V) £5.50, Thai
Green Curry (V) £5.50
Opening Hours: Monday - Saturday noon - 3pm & 6pm - 9pm
(food) Sunday 12.30pm - 3pm & 7pm - 9pm

The Marina

Brighton Pagoda Oriental Restaurant

West Quay, Brighton Marina BN2 5UF
Tel: 01273 819053

Type of Cuisine: Oriental

Breakdown: (out of 60 dishes) Vegetarian: 30%; Vegan: 20%

This restaurant is actually in the marina itself and it floats!
It's the big green and red boat and it's worth a visit just for
that. The food is good too!

Vegetarian Spring Rolls £3, Sal-le Pepe Bean Curd £4,
Vegetarian Hot & Sour Soup £3, Aubergines in Sea Spiced
Sauce £6, Quick Fried Mange Tout in Garlic £5

Opening Hours: Every day noon - 11pm

Café Paradiso

Brighton Marina BN2 5WA
Tel: 01273 665444

Type of Cuisine: Global

Breakdown: (out of 31 dishes) Vegetarian: 30%; Vegan: 10%

This place has a very strange décor of beehives (but no bees)
with big silver tubes coming out of them, and up across the
ceiling there's lots of bamboo and a big white dome in the
middle of the restaurant which is the wood burning oven. It
sounds odd, but it works. The menu is creative too!

Yellow Tomato Soup with Basil Oil £4.25, Baked Ricotta &
Rocket Salad with Sweet Red Onion £6.50, Parpardelle Pasta
with Wild Mushrooms, Baby Asparagus, Crispy Shallots &
Sussex Parmesan £9.95, Halloumi & Shallot Tarte Tatin with
Tomato Pesto & Rocket Salad £7.95

Opening Hours: Monday - Friday noon - 3pm & 7pm - 10pm

Saturday & Sunday 12.30pm - 3.30pm & 7pm - 10pm

El Patio

7 Waterfront, Brighton Marina BN2 5WA
Tel: 01273 607700

Type of Cuisine: Tapas

Breakdown: (out of 60 dishes) Vegetarian: 30%; Vegan: 20%

On a sunny day you could sit outside on the deck of El Patio, sampling tapas and overlooking the boats and convince yourself you're in Spain. There's plenty of vegan and vegetarian choices, it's good to order a few and share.
Alcachofas Marinades (V) (artichokes marinated in lemon juice, olive oil & peppers) £3.70, Pimientos Asados con Ajo (V) (roasted peppers with garlic, olive oil & balsamic vinegar) £3.70, Calabacino Fritos (courgettes fried in breadcrumbs) £3.40, Patatas Bravas (sauté potatoes in a spicy tomato sauce)

Opening Hours: Every day 11am - 11pm

Emperor of China

Unit 8, Waterfront, Brighton Marina BN2 5WA
Tel: 01273 686833

Type of Cuisine: Chinese

Breakdown: (out of 150 dishes) Vegetarian: 20%; Vegan: 15%

This is a great venue for large parties, you can all sit round the big round tables and share tasty morsels. They have mock duck (freaks me out every time but I still keep trying it!) and a good selection vegetables and bean curd in whatever sauce does it for you, make mine a sweet & sour.
Chinese Mushrooms & Bamboo Shoots £4.50, Kung-Po Chilli Bean Curd £5, Sweet & Sour Bean Curd £5, Vegetarian Set Menu (crispy spring rolls, seaweed, skewed courgettes, satay samosa, vegetarian crispy duck, bean curd with cashew nuts in

yellow bean sauce, vegetarian sweet & sour chicken, monks
vegetables & fried noodles with beansprouts) £12 per person
Opening Hours: Monday - Thursday noon - 11.30pm
Friday & Saturday noon - 12pm
Sunday & Bank Holidays noon - 11.30pm

Frankie & Benny's

3 Waterfront, Brighton Marina BN2 5WA
Tel: 01273 688450
Type of Cuisine: New York Italian
Breakdown: (out of 50 dishes) Vegetarian: 20%; Vegan: 10%
*A warm welcome combined with generous Italian-American
fodder make this place a popular choice. The green and
brown décor offers a cosy feel even though it's a large
venue. Lots of the veggie dishes are heavy on the cheese but
don't be put off and ask about the vegan options.*
Mushroom Calzone £6.95, Mozzarella & Tomato Salad £3.45,
Mushroom Ravioli £7.95, Potato Skins with Cheese & Chive
£3.95, Aubergine Parmigana (aubergine layered with
mozzarella & neapolitan sauce) with Fries £7.95
Opening Hours: Monday - Saturday noon - 11pm
Sunday noon - 10.30pm

M A Potters

Waterfront, Brighton Marina BN2 5WA
Tel: 01273 686821
Type of Cuisine: Char-grill
Breakdown: (out of 60 dishes) Vegetarian: 20%; Vegan: 10%
*There's another fantastic view out over the marina from
this café-style restaurant. The food is reasonably priced and
plentiful. Although there's nothing specifically vegan on
the menu if you let them know they'll cater for you. There's*

*vegetarian goodies throughout the menu and a vegetarian
section on the lunchtime menu which is also available in
the evenings.*

Mexican Veggie Chinichanga (deep-fried flour tortillas
stuffed with feta cheese, mushrooms, peppers & pesto on
savoury rice) £8.55, Vegetarian Breakfast £5.25,
Mediterranean Risotto £8.55, Veggie Burger £6.95
Opening Hours: Monday - Wednesday 9am - 10.30pm
Thursday - Saturday 9am - 11pm Sunday 9am - 10pm

Pizza Express

Unit 4, Waterfront, Brighton Marina BN2 5WA
Tel: 01273 689300

Type of Cuisine: Italian
Breakdown: (out of 50 dishes) Vegetarian: 25%; Vegan: 20%
*Pizza Express is situated in an airy glassy building shaped a
bit like a boat and looking out over the boats of the marina.
As a company Pizza Express are vegan and allergy-aware.
They have a booklet in each shop which tells the staff what
diets each dish is suitable for. Their pizza bases are vegan so
just pick your toppings and tell them to hold off on the
cheese. So enjoy a pizza while listening to the clinking of
sails – bliss!*

Garlic Bread £1.95, Bruschetta (freshly baked bread with red
onions, tomatoes, garlic & fresh basil pesto) £3.25, Baked
Dough Balls £1.95, Veneziana Pizza (onions, capers, olives,
sultanas & pine kernels) £5.55, Caprina Pizza (goat's cheese &
sun-dried tomatoes) £6.95
Opening Hours: Every day 11.30am - 11pm

Shops
Brighton

Brighton is full of funky and fabulous shops. Head to the Lanes for jewellery, antiques and unusual gifts. Seek out retro clothes, records and designer furniture in the North Laine. Alternatively check out Churchill Square for all the high street chains. Listed below are a few of me faves!

Aveda Pure-Fumerie

8 Dukes Lane, Brighton BN1 1BG
Tel: 01273 720203
W: www.aveda.com
Aveda's mission is to care for the world we live in, from the products they make to the ways in which they give back to society. They strive to set an example for environmental responsibility and most of their products are vegan. Aveda make hair care products seeing you through from cleansing to finishing, they also make hair colours. They use plant ingredients and aromas to soothe you as well as to treat your hair.
Cruelty-free: Products not tested on animals.
Opening Hours: Monday - Friday 9.30am - 5.50pm
Sunday noon - 5pm

Bill's @ The Depot

100 North Road, Brighton BN1 1YE
Tel: 01273 692894
W: www.billsproducestore.co.uk
Bill's sells high quality speciality foods. There's loads of fresh

and unusual vegetables, herbs and fruits as well as luxury store cupboard goodies and beautifully wrapped biscuits for pressies (or just to scoff yourself!). There's also a bustling café at the back of the shop.

Opening Hours: Monday - Saturday 8am - 7pm
Sunday 10am - 4pm

Blackout

53 Kensington Place, Brighton BN1 4EJ
Tel: 01273 671741

Fabulously funky things! Beautifully hand-crafted bags, clothes, beads and bobbles and some amazing incense decorate this den of delight. The cards are very unusual, recycled and right on. Goods are from all over the planet – discovered by an environmentally conscious collective. Blackout is well worth a visit.

Enviro: Carrier bags are made from recycled paper, waste is recycled and recycled stationery is used. The Blackout products are made by women's co-operatives and are fairly traded.

Opening Hours: Monday - Saturday 10am - 6pm

Brighton Peace & Environment Centre

39-41 Surrey Street, Brighton BN1 3PB
Tel: 01273 766610

An ethical trade shop with a library and educational unit. Located close to the station, the Peace & Environment Centre is run entirely by volunteers who work really hard. For ethical pressies, this is the place. It sells t-shirts, stationery, books, journals, cards, crafts and gifts from organisations working for peace, justice and environmental protection.

Cruelty-free: Sell a variety of vegetarian and vegan books.
Enviro: Recycles packaging etc and fundraises for

environmental organisations.
Opening Hours: Monday - Saturday 10am - 5.30pm
Sunday closed

Evolution

> *42 Bond Street, Brighton BN1 1RD*
> *Tel: 01273 205379*
> *E: evolution@evobond.freeserve.co.uk*
> *& 89 Western Road, Brighton BN1 2LB*
> *Tel: 01273 727123*

Gift shop. Evolution is a Buddhist Right Livelihood Business. They aim to help Buddhists to work together and all profits go to charitable projects in Britain and abroad. They sell candles, household items, books, cards, essential oils and many other goodies. Evolution shops can be found dotted around the country and each one is a treasure chest of fascinating bits and bobs. Brighton has the luxury of two Evolution shops, and both are delightful.

Cruelty-free: Tries to ensure that all products are produced without cruelty to animals.

Enviro: All used cardboard and packaging is recycled and they encourage customers to re-use bags. Aims to ensure that all goods are environmentally sound and that producers are paid a fair price for their work.

Opening Hours: (Bond Street) Monday - Saturday 10am - 5.30pm Sunday noon - 5:30pm
(Western Road) Monday - Saturday 10am - 6pm Sunday 11am - 5pm

Health Link

21f Station Road, Portslade, Brighton BN41 1GX
Tel: 01273 420120

High street health shop. Health Link is an independent health shop with qualified product advisors. They specialise in vegetarian and vegan foods, organic foods, vitamin and mineral supplements, herbal and homeopathic remedies and cruelty-free cosmetics.
Cruelty-free: Beauty Without Cruelty products etc.
Enviro: Recycle waste, re-use carrier bags and use recycled stationery.
Opening Hours: Monday - Saturday 9am - 5.30pm

The Hemp Shop

19 Gardner Street, Brighton BN1 1UP
Tel: 01273 818047

Originally a mail order set up and now with a shop here in Brighton, The Hemp Shop sells stationery, books, beauty products clothing and food. You can also get advice here on hemp nutrition.
Opening Hours: Monday - Saturday 10am - 5.30pm

Hocus Pocus

38 Gardner Street, Brighton BN1 1UN
Tel: 01273 572212

A very different kind of shop – a 'creative lifestyle shop' encouraging the work of quality crafts people. Hocus Pocus is very popular – no doubt partly due to the positive attitude of the two women who run it. Hocus Pocus has managed to slip into the gap between hippydom and super cool – it is New Age and alternative selling Tarot cards, crystals, grain incenses, legal highs and daily tarot consultations. A huge range of products are available here from angelic artefacts to alien lifeforms and aromatherapy.

Opening Hours: Monday - Saturday 9am - 7.30pm (May - Sept) 10am - 6pm (Oct - April)
Sunday 11am - 6pm (May - Sept) noon - 4.30pm (Oct - April)

Infinity Foods Co-operative

25 North Road, Brighton BN1 1YA
Tel: 01273 603563

Central Brighton's excellent wholefood shop specialises in vegetarian, vegan and organic foods – including fruit and veg, pulses, herbs, pates and much more. Also has its own bakery and sells a wide variety of breads. Offers refilling service for all sorts of products – apple juice, toilet cleaner, laundry liquid, tamari etc. Money saving large sizes available. Retailers/trade can order products in bulk direct from Infinity Foods Wholesale – contact the warehouse at: 67 Norway Street, Portslade; tel: 01273 424060.

Cruelty-free: Specialise in vegan, vegetarian and organic produce.

Enviro: Recycle all paper and cardboard.

Opening Hours: Monday - Thursday & Saturday 9.30am - 5.30pm Friday 9.30am - 6pm

Kemptown Deli

108 St George's Road, Brighton BN2 1EA
Tel: 01273 603411

Type of Cuisine: Deli Cheeses, Bread, Olives, Biscuits, Juices and Pasties

Breakdown: (out of 100s of dishes) Vegetarian: 60%; Vegan: 2%

The Kemptown Deli has an amazing range of cheeses, pasties, sandwiches, breads, jams and biscuits. They also sell fresh home-made pesto and organic juices such as apple & cinnamon juice.

Mature Farmhouse Cheddar Cheese & Crisp Apple Sandwich £1.60, Vegetable Pakora 75p, Apple & Cinnamon Juice £2.25, Spinach & Cream Cheese Pasty 90p

Opening Hours: Monday - Saturday 9am - 6pm

Lush   ✔ 10%

41 East Street, Brighton BN1 1HL
Tel: 01273 774700
W: www.lush.co.uk

Mmmmmmmm! Lush sells totally yummy hand-made body products. Seriously scrumptious bath bombs, soaps, massage bars, shampoos, moisturisers – I guarantee you'll want the lot. If you have trouble finding Lush use your snoot – the scents totally pervade the street. Loads of their products are vegan – either look in the Lush Times or ask a member of staff, they're always really helpful.

Opening Hours: Monday - Saturday 9am - 6pm
Sunday 11am - 5pm

Montezuma's Chocolates

 10%

15 Duke Street, Brighton BN1 1AH
Tel: 01273 324979
E: sales@montezumas.co.uk
W: www.montezumas.co.uk

Type of Cuisine: Chocolate, Truffles and Fudge
Gob-smackingly scrumptious treats, loads of which are vegan. I guarantee you'll be overwhelmed by the selection. The cocoa they use comes from co-operative organisations in the Dominican Republic, so it's ethically sourced. The treats are beautifully displayed and packaged, making ideal gifts.
Opening Hours: Monday - Saturday 9.30am - 6.30pm Sunday noon - 5pm

Pulse

The Open Market, London Road, Brighton BN1 1JS
Tel: 01273 693355

This is a must for the wholefood bargain hunter. It's where I try and do all my shopping these days. You can scoop and weigh all your nuts, pulses, muesli and grains, buy locally produced organic fruit, veg and bread, refill your eco cleaning product bottles and get vegan chocolate here! What more could you ask for?
Opening Hours: Monday, Tuesday, Thursday - Saturday 9am - 5pm Wednesday 9am - 1pm Sunday - Closed

Sunny Foods

76 Beaconsfield Road, Brighton BN1 6DD
Tel: 01273 507879

Animal and people friendly! Sunny Foods promotes vegan and organic foods and endeavours to keep its prices low. Products include health foods, organic fruit and vegetables, organic foods and vegan specialities. The shop is quite a way out from the central shopping area of Brighton, but it's the best thing since sliced bread for the people who live around Preston Park and its long opening hours make it a great place for emergency vegan ice-cream and chocolate.
Cruelty-free: Specialises in vegan and organic foods.
Enviro: Recycle whenever possible and sell no genetically modified products.
Opening Hours: Every day 8am - 8pm

Taj Natural Foods

95 Western Road, Brighton BN1 2LB
Tel: 01273 325027

This is a dream supermarket (apart from the meat counter at the back). You can find a wide selection of vegan goodies from sausages and haggis to chocolate as well as a wealth of world cuisine. There's plenty of fresh vegetables and herbs, dried spices and pulses and a deli counter for falafel. This really is the place of culinary inspiration. They also sell eco cleaning and beauty products.
Opening Hours: Monday - Sunday 8.30am - 9.30pm

Traid (Textile Recycling for Aid & International Development)

39 Duke Street, Brighton BN1 1AG
Tel: 01273 746346
W: www.traid.org.uk

Traid is a charity committed to combating world poverty by recycling at home. Funds raised in the UK through the collection and sale of second-hand clothing and shoes further sustainable development in some of the poorest regions of the world. They sell groovy recycled gear including retro clothing, designer wear and one-off items along with casual wear and children's clothes. Get yourself a unique outfit for under £20 and save the world while you're at it!

Opening Hours: Monday - Saturday 10am - 6pm
Sunday 11am - 5pm

Tucan

29 Bond Street, Brighton BN1 1RD
Tel: 01273 326351
E: tucancraft@dial.pipex.com

Fair trade shop with Latin America. Tucan has a wide range of authentic exotic artefacts for that special gift. They specialise in furniture and crafts, clothing and jewellery.

Opening Hours: Every day 10am - 5.30pm

Vegetarian Shoes

12 Gardner Street, Brighton BN1 1UP
Tel: 01273 691913
W: www.vegetarian-shoes.co.uk
Vegetarian shoes, jackets and accessories. Vegetarian Shoes sells wait for it... vegetarian shoes, among other things. If you haven't already ordered from them by mail then pop in and choose from a fantastic and large selection of footwear. Whether you're after breathable trainers, dainty court shoes or knee length biker boots you'll find them here and they're top quality.
Cruelty-free: Yes. (Sells vegan shoes, boots, jackets, bags, t-shirts, belts, wallets.)
Enviro: Recycles cardboard packaging.
Opening Hours: Monday - Saturday 10am - 5.30pm

Winfalcon Healing Centre & Shop

28-29 Ship Street, Brighton BN1 1AD
Tel: 01273 728997
E: winfalcon@dial.pipex.com
Complementary therapies, readings, channelling, natural remedies, aura imaging, holistic shop, crystals. If you have come to Brighton for the New Age healing vibes then head for Winfalcon for your fix.
Cruelty-free: Nothing is tested on animals. Sells aloe vera products, flower remedies, crystals etc.
Enviro: Recycle paper where possible, re-use bags and boxes. Use recycled products where possible.
Opening Hours: Monday - Friday 10am - 5.30pm
Saturday 10am - 6pm Sunday noon - 4pm

Lewes

Full Of Beans

96-97 High Street, Lewes BN7 1XH
Tel: 01273 472627

*Wholefood shop. Established in 1978 by Sarah and John,
they manufacture their own tofu, tempeh and miso from
organic soya beans and provide a large range of organic
dairy and sheep products as well as special diet products.
They also do an organic vegetable box scheme.*

Cruelty-free: Specialises in vegetarian foods.

Enviro: Accept carrier bags for re-use and recycle egg boxes.

Opening Hours: Monday - Saturday 9am - 5.30pm

Landsdown Health Foods

44 Cliffe High Street, Lewes BN7 2AN
Tel: 01273 474681

*Health food shop. Sells a wide range of organic and
wholefoods as well as herbal remedies, cosmetics, books and
household goods. Operates with ethical principles and offers
helpful, qualified advice.*

Cruelty-free: Yes – specialises in veggie foods and cruelty-
free cosmetics.

Enviro: Re-use carrier bags, ask before giving bags away and
use all environmentally-friendly cleaning products.

Opening Hours: Monday - Saturday 9am - 5.30pm

National Chains

The Body Shop

41-43 North Street, Brighton BN1 1RH
Tel: 01273 327048
& 22 George Street, Hove BN3 3YA
Tel: 01273 724481
& 80 Montague Street, Worthing BN11 3HF
Tel: 01903 214369

Holland & Barrett

105 London Road, Brighton BN1 4JG
Tel: 01273 696209
& 66-68 North Street, Brighton BN1 1RH
Tel: 01273 746343
& 68 George Street, Hove BN3 3YD
Tel: 01273 321873
& 11 Warwick Street, Worthing BN11 3DF
Tel: 01903 231274

GNC

Unit 43, Churchill Square, Brighton BN1 2TD
Tel: 01273 710150

Useful phone numbers

Viva!:	0117 944 1000
Tourist Information:	0906 7112255
National Rail Enquiries:	08457 484950
National Express Coaches:	0870 5808080
Brighton & Hove Cabs:	01273 204060
Brighton Streamline Taxis:	01273 747474
Mile Oak Taxis:	01273 420460
Southern Streamline:	01273 775544
Southern Taxis:	01273 205205
Streamline Taxis:	01273 202020

By road – Brighton is approx 60 miles from London via
A23/M23

Index

Shops

Viva la *Viva!*

campaigning for...

animals

In Britain, almost a billion animals are brutally slaughtered for meat every year. Very few farmed animals reach the natural end of their lifespan and are usually killed when they are babies. In the short life they do have the overwhelming majority are exploited, neglected and frustrated on factory farms – there only to produce a profit – before meeting a violent, frightening death in the slaughterhouse.

the environment

The tone of major reports has become desperate as the decline of the natural world accelerates – a thousand times faster than at any point in its history. Livestock production is at the heart of the decline: erosion, spreading deserts, torched rainforests and pollution. And the seas are on the point of ecological collapse.

people

Every year, millions of people die from hunger alongside fields of fodder destined for the West's livestock.

health

Cancer, heart disease, strokes, diabetes and a string of other degenerative diseases – linked to modern, meat-based, Western lifestyles – are destroying our health and blighting our children's future. Vegetarians suffer less from disease and live longer, yet it's animal products that are subsidised, promoted and encouraged.

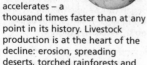

115

Viva! making a difference...

Pig in hell

We revealed the myth that British is best is a load of pork pies after exposing appalling conditions in pig farms throughout the UK.

Doing it for ducks

Our campaigns against duck farming were responsible for cutting the sale of factory farmed duck meat.

Sacred cows
We lifted the lid on modern dairy farming, publicising the mental and physical suffering inflicted on millions of cows and their calves every year.

Exotic meats
Our campaign has led to all the large supermarket chains and many independent retailers dumping the sale of meat from wild animals, such as kangaroo.

Going for the kill
Disturbing footage shot secretly inside slaughterhouses blew the myth that animals are killed humanely.

No more excuses
Our dynamic youth campaign put an end to all the ifs and buts and showed there really is no excuse for not going veggie!

That's the way to do it!

We have helped millions of people go veggie and vegan through our colourful *It's Time To Go Veggie* magazine and ongoing tour of Incredible Veggie Roadshows.

...and more

For up-to-date campaign info, events listings, recipes for every occasion, to shop online for vegan chocs and sweeties, t-shirts, gifts, toiletries and books, go to: www.viva.org.uk

---

Add your voice to ours to make us e

Join Viva!

Supporter £15/£12 unwaged
You'll receive our tri-yearly magazine *Viva!LIFE*, packed with campaign info, recipes, global news on animals, the environment and health, celebrity interviews and giveaways of new vegan products. Plus, a Supporter's card, getting you great discounts off hundreds of veggie shops, services, restaurants and holidays in the UK, Ireland and abroad.

Star Supporter £25
As well as *Viva!LIFE* and a Supporter's card, you'll get our *Not in my Name* celebrity DVD (also includes 'The Viva! 10' campaign films), six Viva! Guides including *Martin Shaw Cooks Veggie*, a special certificate, Viva! brooch and sticker.

Activist (under 18s) £5
Activists get stickers, posters and their own mini-mag *Viva!ACTIVE* three times a year, choc full of competitions, quizzes, easy peasy recipes, letters, penpals and the latest animal news!

"Join Viva! now and help us spread the word against the cruelties done against animals in the name of diet." **Sir Paul McCartney**

"The scale of abuse in Britain's farms is a national disgrace. Please support Viva!'s campaigns to end the torture." **Chrissie Hynde**

"Supporting Viva! means saving animals from suffering – join Viva!." **Jeremy Cunningham, The Levellers**

e effective: Join Us!... see over page

YES, I'd like to join Viva! as a

☐ Supporter £15/£12

☐ Star Supporter £25

☐ Activist £5

☐ YES, I'd like to make a donation to help the animals and enclose £ _____

☐ I enclose a cheque/PO payable to Viva!

☐ Please debit my Visa/Switch/Maestro/Mastercard:

Expiry Date: ____/____ Start Date/Issue No ____/____

Title _____ First Name _____

Surname _____

Address _____

_____

_____ Postcode _____

Tel _____

Date of Birth (if under 18) _____

Viva!

Return to Viva!, 8 York Court, Wilder Street, Bristol BS2 8QH; or call 0117 944 1000 (Mon-Fri 9am-6pm); or join online at www.viva.org.uk

Notes

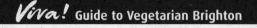

Notes